latch–hooking
rugs

latch-hooking rugs

rugs

Lynda Spiro

A & C Black ■ London
University of Pennsylvania Press ■ Philadelphia

Dedication

For Michael, Mark and James. Amongst other things, thank you for your patience,
help, interest, enthusiasm, support and unconditional love.

And for my Dad, who I know would have been so proud.

First published in Great Britain in 2008
A & C Black Publishers Limited
38 Soho Square
London W1D 3HB
www.acblack.com

ISBN-13: 978-0-7136-8543-5

Published simultaneously in the USA by
University of Pennsylvania Press
3905 Spruce Street
Philadelphia, Pennsylvania 19104-4112
www.pennpress.org

ISBN 978-0-8122-2043-8

CIP Catalogue records for this book are available
from the British Library and the U.S. Library of
Congress.

Book design: Susan McIntyre
Cover design: Sutchinda Rangsi Thompson
Photography: Adrian Pope
Commissioning Editor: Susan Kelly

Printed and bound in China

This book is produced using paper that is made
from wood grown in managed, sustainable forests.
It is natural, renewable and recyclable. The logging
and manufacturing processes conform to the
environmental regulations of the country of origin.

The author and publisher cannot accept any
liability for the use or misuse of any materials or
equipment mentioned in this book. Always read
any product and equipment instructions and take
any necessary precautions.

contents

ACKNOWLEDGEMENTS

Big thanks to the following individuals and organisations for their help in the creation of this book:

Susan Kelly, my wonderful editor. Thanks for asking me to write this book and for believing in me when I said that I would and could do it. Where would I be without your invaluable advice and incredible sense of humour?

I don't think that this book would have happened had it not been for Jeff Bowskill, the Managing Director of Readicut. Thanks for giving me Be's phone number way back in the very beginning, and for then introducing me to Donald Mcmillan, the Operations Director at Coats Crafts UK who handed me over to Jill Rushton; Jill not only organised, processed and delivered the wool and canvas for the rugs in this book, but also allowed me to interpret one of her son Jack's paintings as a rug.

The talented and exceptional Be: thank you for your invaluable contribution and support; this book would not have seen the light of day without your enthusiasm and encouragement, and I am eternally grateful.

To my friends (who I hope are still my friends after this process) and my family (who will always be my family): I can now come out and play again, having finished 'doing the book'. Thanks for your support and encouragement throughout.

To everyone's favourite photographer: Adrian Pope. Thank you for your skill, suggestions and patience.

To Yasmin, my lovely cousin and my hand model; thanks for picking up latch-hooking so quickly and beautifully.

Thanks also to my hooker-helpers (you don't honestly think that I made them all myself?), for following instructions carefully and for working quickly to get them all finished.

All the wool used in this book has been supplied and manufactured by Anchor. (Their generous contribution of the finest quality wool and rug canvas is much appreciated.)

GETTING HOOKED

Craft is making a comeback. Traditional crafts have always had a following, but it is now fashionable again to buy and even make your own 'crafty' home accessories (along with loads of other things). This revival of interest in the crafts and in hand-skills is known in some circles as 'traditionalising'. Crafts that had slipped out of the trendy spotlight for a while are now more popular than ever; are we all reacting against mass-market, identical products and the throwaway society, or are we just remembering the joy and pride inherent in working with our hands to create beautiful, one-of-a-kind, decorative pieces, and in being able to say 'I made it myself'? Latch-hooking is now often referred to as a 'vintage craft', but I don't want to overanalyse the rise and fall of such trends and their sociological significance here – suffice to say, it is wonderful that a passion for making is being rekindled in so many different craft areas and it is exciting to be able to share some of my latch-hooking tips with you in this book.

Remember the 1970s craze for latch-hooked rugs? After a bit of a break whilst other crafts took centre-stage, latch-hooking is the latest old school craft to enjoy a revival; it is cool, kitsch, fun and amazingly easy to do – think painting by numbers using pieces of coloured wool instead of paint. Latch-hooking your own rugs is a simple, creative, cost effective and versatile way to change the look of an interior, and importantly is it fun and easy as well. Once you have had a taste, I guarantee you will be hooked; it is a relaxing pastime and fun for all ages and abilities. Most importantly, you can learn to latch-hook in just a few simple steps.

Whether their first role is practical or decorative, rugs must incorporate the right colour and shape balances to appeal to those who live with them and to complement various components of the room. I believe in drawing on colours from nature and translating these colour themes into rugs; nature has its own way of tempering colour to convey emotion, and mimicking these in the home helps create a sense of comfort and well-being. With that in mind, the rug patterns featured in this book have all been designed to be, above all, bright, happy and fun.

Over the years while my grandmother crocheted, my mother knitted, and my sister embroidered, I, as the youngest, latch-hooked – I loved it from day one. When I was asked to write a book on rugs my initial reaction was pure joy at being able to share the pleasure of this craft with so many new people – such an exciting prospect. I hope that you enjoy catching the latch-hooking bug and hook yourself some beautiful rugs to be proud of.

INTRODUCTION

A latch-hook is a combination of a hand hook and a latchet, derived from knitting machines in the mid-1920s. Latch-hooking became particularly popular as a technique in the mid-'30s, because of its simplicity and versatility.

Rugs have served as an essential part of home interiors for thousands of years, serving both practical and aesthetic functions. In the beginning, rugs gave essential warmth and protection from the elements as well as providing visual features. Animal hides provided the first flooring, sitting and sleeping surfaces and covers. As our societies have developed, we have become better protected from the elements; our homes are more secure and we enjoy more leisure and luxury. The function of rugs has progressed past their purely practical function and they are now decorative vehicles for artistic expression as well as simple floor coverings.

I have always felt that decorating with rugs can usually be categorised in three different ways. The first is to use the rug purely as a focal point. The second is serving as a home décor accessory, tying in with other elements of the interior. The third category is employing the rug mainly in its practical role. Perhaps, even more importantly, rugs are a relatively quick and easy way to update the interior's look, transforming a room without the complicated hassle of redecorating. A room can also be divided easily through the careful use of rugs when it is not possible to physically divide the space with walls or furniture. Rugs can add softness and interest to hard floors.

You don't have to restrict your rugs to the floor though – you can hang special rugs on the wall to make a striking statement, in just the same way as you would use a painting. Remember, whether you decide to hang, drape, or lay your latch-hooking efforts, the addition of such a unique, one-off piece of handmade work to your home is something to display with pride.

why latch-hook?

There are so many different reasons for wanting to latch-hook. Personally, I find it relaxing and therapeutic, as it gives me the chance to sit and work with my hands for a while; this can be an amazing luxury within today's fast-paced lifestyles, but it is just so important to make time to recharge your energy with creative activities somehow. The repetitive movement of latch-hooking can be a great stress reliever – in many ways, the emotional benefits are similar to those of meditation. Also, let's not forget the huge positive boost of personal satisfaction when you complete a project.

Portability is a plus too. When you are creating a latch-hooking project, you can take it with you and continue work on the bus, in the doctor's waiting room, even during your lunch hour. You can latch-hook for a few minutes here and there – even if you don't have large chunks of spare time in your day you can make little windows of latch-hooking opportunities while watching television, talking with your family, sitting in the garden, waiting for a cake to bake, or listening to the radio. You don't have to finish the whole rug at a gallop – you can work on a section for a while then come back to it after a few months, working slowly to complete your work carefully and precisely rather than racing to get a project out of the way. You can pick it up and put it down when it suits you.

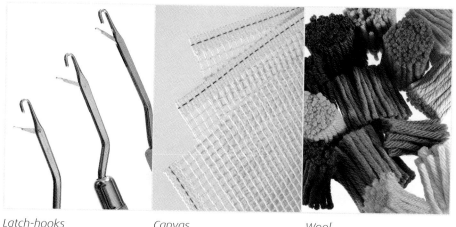

Latch-hooks   Canvas   Wool

The process of latch-hooking couldn't be simpler – you just hook a pre-cut length of wool through woven canvas using the hinged hook. The wool is looped under and around each horizontal canvas thread, resulting in a short strong knot. The process of creating a whole rug does take time – no instant gratification here. But the time and effort that you put in are a big part of what makes this kind of work so special, and making your own rug (or rugs for family and friends) will give you a real sense of achievement.

One tool   *One knot*

In terms of equipment and techniques, one simple tool and one easily-learned knot are really all it takes to get you hooking. The latch-hook tool is strong and easy to use, and even if you do happen to make a mistake, you can very easily undo one knot and reuse the wool – just think of it as getting extra practice.

02 equipment and materials

LATCH-HOOK

You only need one tool for latch-hooking but there are several varieties to choose from. All latch-hooks are made of a steel hook and latchet. The stem of the hook may be either straight or curved, and the handle of the hook can be either wooden or 'bendy'. Personally, I prefer to hook with a straight-stemmed tool with a wooden handle – the old fashioned way – as this is how I was taught to work. But different hookers prefer different tools, and I would suggest that you experiment with both types and various different brands to find your own favourite type of hook.

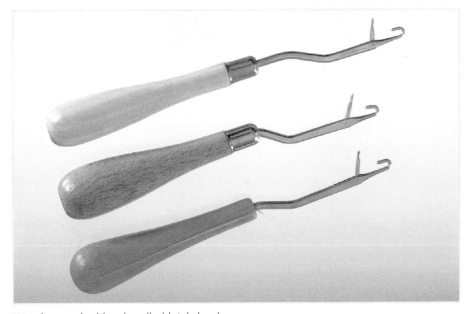

Wooden- and rubber-handled latch-hooks

CANVAS

The canvas used for latch-hooking has an open mesh of double threads with approximately 3 holes to 2.5cm (1 in.) of canvas. Look at the canvas closely and you will see that it is woven with double horizontal threads and twisted vertical threads. The knots are made over the double horizontal threads. Each hole on the canvas will be used to house one knot.

Canvas is available to buy in a variety of widths and you then cut it to your desired length. This means that whilst the edges on each side are properly finished with a woven selvedge, there will be a raw edge at both the top and bottom of your piece. Raw edges are dealt with in the Finishing section (p.117). Don't forget, when you trim your canvas, to leave an extra four holes at each end for finishing.

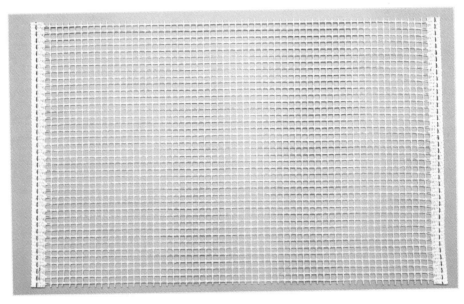

Canvas

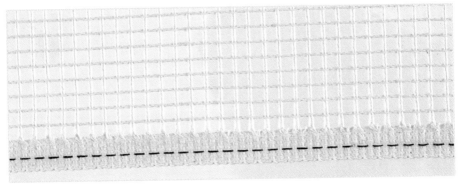

Close-up of selvedge-bound canvas

Wonderful wool

WOOL

Rug wool is available either by the hank (skein) or in ready-cut lengths of approximately 6.5cm (2½ in.). I have used ready-cut lengths of wool for all the designs in this book. If you prefer to cut your own lengths, choose something like Rowan Big Wool 80m/100g skeins of 100% wool (bulky weight) available from www.knitrowan.com.

BINDING TAPE

Binding tape is available from any good haberdashery shop or craft supplier. (See Suppliers on p.142.) Heavy-duty cotton tape (approximately 4cm (1½ in.) wide) is also available. I try to avoid using binding tape too often as I do find it quite fiddly. But when I do use it, I prefer to use the cotton-tape type that requires sewing on by hand as opposed to the self adhesive one that seems to un-stick very quickly.

Binding tape

STRONG THREAD

Use a strong linen thread when sewing binding tape onto the back of finished pieces. This thread is available from any good haberdashery shop or craft supplier. (See Suppliers on p.142.)

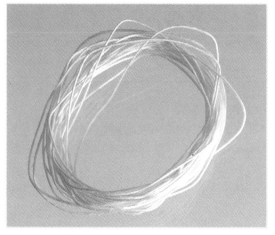

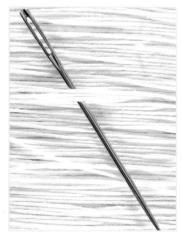

Linen thread

Sharp needle and strong thread

SHARP SEWING NEEDLE

You may already have plenty of needles in your sewing box, but if you don't you can buy them at the supermarket, in department stores, in hardware shops and of course haberdashery shops and craft suppliers.

FRINGING WOOL

I like to use double knitting wool (2-ply) cut to size.

2-ply wool suitable for fringing

methods and techniques

BINDING

Before you start, the first thing to do (apart from making sure you have everything you need) is to decide on the binding method you want to use. If you are going to bind the edges once the latch-hooking is complete, then carry on from here and refer to the section on pp. 118-120. However, you may want to choose the quick and easy option of binding the edges as you hook. I often use this method when the canvas has four raw edges, and find this a very neat and quick way of finishing off my rugs, particularly when I am hooking the smaller pieces of canvas (such as the 12-in. square pieces). The photos probably explain what to do better than the words. So this is how I do it:

1 Starting at the top raw edge. Fold under four extra rows of canvas beyond the end of the design. Work these four extra rows through the double thickness to prevent the canvas unravelling.

2 After having completed the first four rows, fold under the extra four rows at both sides of the piece. From the fourth row down, work the four extra rows double thickness at each side of the piece as you hook horizontally across the design.

3 By having only hooked the raw edges on the verticals from the fourth row down, you will see that you have created a small unhooked square in each corner.

4 When nearing completion, fold under the extra four rows at the bottom end and work through the double thickness.

5 The four raw ends of your piece of canvas are now securely locked in and no binding will be needed.

A completed square made using the 'bind as you hook' method

HOOKING METHODS

There are two different methods of latch-hooking. Either can be used if only one person is hooking a rug, but, whether you choose the first or second option, this method must be consistently used throughout so that all the knots will lie in the same direction. If two people are working on one very large rug, one person must hook using Method 1 on one end and the other using Method 2 on the other end in order to keep the pile in the same direction.

If the canvas has been painted, make sure that you are preparing to work with the painted side face up. The wool should be knotted onto the double threads of the canvas that run horizontally from woven selvedge to woven selvedge. Do not knot on the vertical twisted threads.

However tempting it may be to work each colour section separately, it is very important that you complete the rows horizontally. Starting at one raw end, fold under four extra rows of canvas beyond the end of the design. Work one row at a time, either left to right, or right to left. Complete each row of knots before starting the next. As they say, a picture tells a thousand words, so have a look at the photos with their explanations alongside and start hooking.

If you find your wool is getting too 'shaggy' as you work, try twisting the ends as you go to stop them unravelling. If this doesn't help, you can always trim the wool once the rug is completed.

METHOD 1

1 Loop a piece of wool in half and place the loop behind the shaft of the hook.

2 Push the hook down through one square of the canvas and up through the one immediately above – until the latch is through. Pull the hook back slightly, just far enough until the latch begins to close.

3 Bring the two ends of wool across and place them into the eye of the hook.

4 Pull the hook back slowly through the loop – and as you do this, the latch will close and grab the wool. When this happens, release the two ends of wool and continue to pull the hook through. You might find it helpful to place the thumb of your free hand against the base of the knot as you continue to pull the hook out.

5 Keep the two ends even and tighten the knot by pulling gently. A slight pull is all that is needed to 'set' the knot.

6 The finished knot.

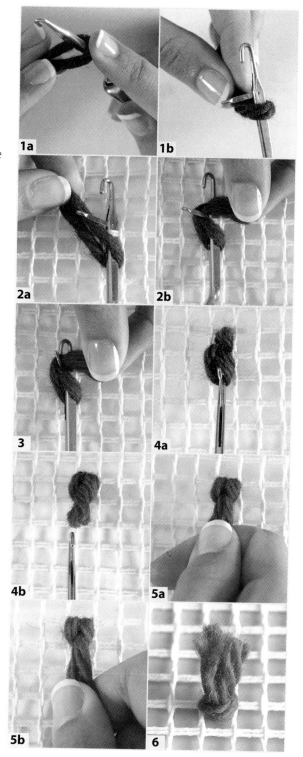

17

METHOD 2

1 Push the hook down through one square of the canvas and up through the one immediately above – until the latch is through. Then catch the loop of a doubled piece of wool in the hook.

2 Pull the hook down until the loop of wool comes under the horizontal canvas thread and up through the hole below.

3 Holding the two ends of wool with your free hand, push the hook and latch back up through the looped wool so that the loop is now around the shaft of the hook. Then bring the two ends of wool across and place them into the eye of the hook.

4 Pull the hook back slowly through the loop – as you do this, the latch will close and grab the wool. When this happens, release the two ends of wool and continue to pull the hook through. You might find it helpful to place the thumb of your free hand against the base of the knot as you continue to pull the hook out.

5 Keep the two ends even and tighten the knot by pulling gently. A slight pull is all that is needed to 'set' the knot.

6 The finished knot.

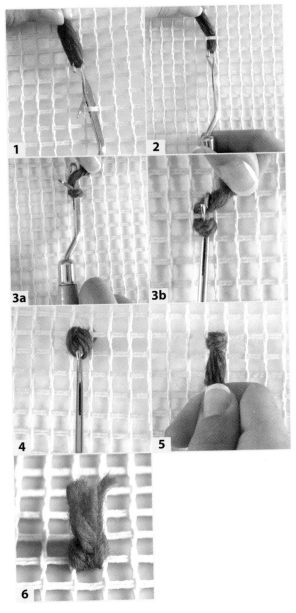

before you begin

The most exciting part of getting started is choosing or creating the design. Choosing the design is the easier option – you just need to look through your pattern options and make a decision about which design and colours you want to use. Creating your own design takes a bit more work: coming up with an idea; thinking about where the rug is ultimately going to be placed (whether it is in your home or someone else's) and considering any relevant colour or light issues arising from its intended position; creating the design; transferring it onto canvas; and laying out all the colours to make sure they work together as you want them to. To get you started though, you should work from the designs I have put together for you in this book. There will be more information about creating your own designs, or simply adapting existing designs, further on in the book once your making skills are developed and you feel more confident and adventurous.

For now though, you should start small – aim to make a little section of a rug design as your first project, just to get the hang of the movement required, and so your hand becomes accustomed to the latch-hook. Later on, you might decide to sew these smaller pieces of practice canvas together to create a larger piece, but for now set yourself this achievable goal, and congratulate yourself when you get there.

To make your first steps easier, I have included a range of tempting patterns, with various colour combinations and options. Remember: these colour suggestions are just that – suggestions. The patterns are like recipes – you can always alter a pattern to suit your own personal taste by replacing suggested colours, like flavours, with your own personal favourites. The selection of designs in this book ranges from simple to more advanced. The choice of where to start is yours. Remember, however simple or sophisticated the design, the technique is always the same: just one tool and one type of knot.

READING CHARTS

The charts will provide you with all the information that you need to complete your rug. Each chart in this book shows the finished rug, with each coloured square on the chart representing a completed knot. The top line of each coloured square in the chart is the position in which you should hook your knot. With a little bit of practice, you will soon be able to read the chart quickly and easily. Before beginning any of the projects in the book, make sure you have everything you need.

SQUARING UP

Making up 12 in. squares should appeal to you new makers. Sometimes it can be a bit off-putting to think about undertaking a large project, but working your rug in small sections is a very practical approach to this seemingly daunting task. Once completed, all the squares are sewn together to make up a complete rug to your own exact specification. Nevertheless, don't feel for one moment that you shouldn't attempt to make the rug on one large piece of canvas if you want to.

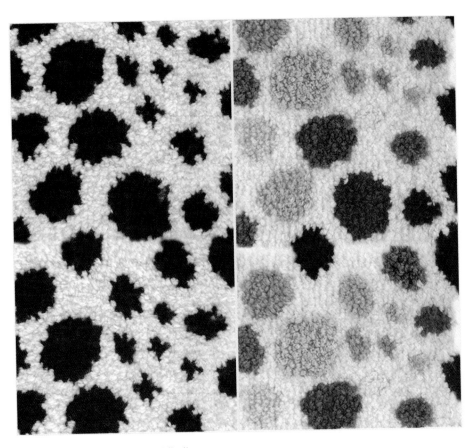

LEFT: *Spots and Dots,* RIGHT: *Oddballs*

POINTS TO REMEMBER

- Before starting to hook, make sure that you have the right size canvas and the correct amounts and colours of wool for any particular project. There is nothing more irritating than running out of wool mid-project.

- Each small square on the chart represents one knot.

- Knot the wool on the double horizontal threads.

- Working either top to bottom on your rug is absolutely fine. But do remember that you must continue in the direction that you start.

- Remember, even if you do happen to make a mistake, it doesn't really matter as one knot is very easy to undo and you can re-use the wool.

- If two people are working on the rug, each must hook in the opposite direction using both of methods to keep the pile of the rug will be consistent.

- Don't be tempted to hook by colours and small areas. The yarn can fray and get dirty as you rub against it when you're hooking the other rug areas.

- Don't wash or tumble dry pure wool rugs; the rugs can be vacuumed as you would any carpet. If a rug does require cleaning, take it to a professional dry cleaners.

- To preserve your rug, treat it with respect. It likes neither stiletto heels nor heavy pieces of furniture.

- Use a cutter gauge for speed and accuracy if cutting your own wool.

- Don't forget that you can include any colours you like and don't have to use the ones that I have recommended.

- Choose all your colours at one time. Lay the colours out, side by side. If one colour looks out of place, substitute it with another until you are happy with your complete colour selection.

- Adding colour to the black and white designs really does change the look of them. It is also a wonderful way of using up those surplus pieces of wool that always seem to find their way to the bottom of the bag. Take a look at Spots and Dots.

- If using canvas without selvedges, use masking tape over the raw edges to prevent fraying.

- Do not wash or tumble dry your pure wool rug.

Soon to Bloom rug, see p.114

rugs to make

TYPES OF STRIPES

Striped rugs are definitely the simplest to work out when it comes to experimenting with individual designs – they are just made up of a few simple lines in a variety of colours and thicknesses. Hooking one of my striped designs as a simple starter project will help make you appreciate how very easy and addictive hooking is. I have created four different striped designs to 'kick start' you into designing your own, with two colourways for each design.

stripe tease

FINISHED SIZE

- Rug: 61cm x 92cm (24 in. x 36 in.) made up from four individual sections each 30cm x 46cm (12 in. x 18 in.)
- Runner: 46cm x 152cm (18 in. x 60 in.) made up from five individual sections each 30cm x 46cm (12 in. x 18 in.).

YOU WILL NEED:

- Latch-hook
- Strong thread
- Sharp sewing needle
- Latch-hook canvas pieces for each individual section, 40 x 60 holes between selvedges, plus selvedge allowance
- 6.5cm (2 ½ in.) lengths of rug wool in the colours below (packs contain approximately 160 pieces).

INSTRUCTIONS

- To bind as you hook, fold under four-hole width at each raw edge. Bind the selvedges through the double canvas at each end as you work.
- Work in horizontal rows, following the chart carefully.
- Turn under and sew bound selvedges to the underside of the completed piece. Finish as desired.

Rug section COLOURWAY 1		30 cm x 46 cm (12 in. x 18 in.)		COLOURWAY 2	30 cm x 46 cm (12 in. x 18 in.)	
Shade	*Code*	*Lengths*	*Packs*	*Shade*		*Code*
Flame Red	(98)	480	4	Sandalwood		(76)
Heather Pink	(52)	960	7	Loam Brown		(28)
Turquoise	(35)	240	2	Light Sand		(87)
Tangerine	(42)	720	5	Tan		(32)

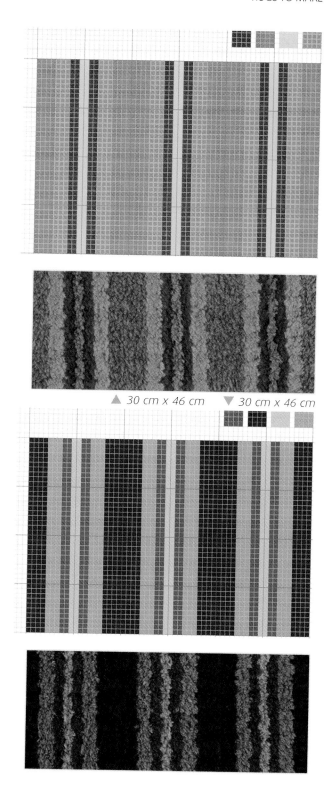

▲ 30 cm x 46 cm   ▼ 30 cm x 46 cm

Rug
COLOURWAY 1

61 cm x 92 cm
(24 in. x 36 in.)

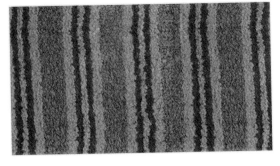

	Shade	Code	Lengths	Packs
	Flame Red	(98)	1920	13
	Heather Pink	(52)	3840	25
	Turquoise	(35)	960	7
	Tangerine	(42)	2880	19

▼ *61 cm x 92 cr*

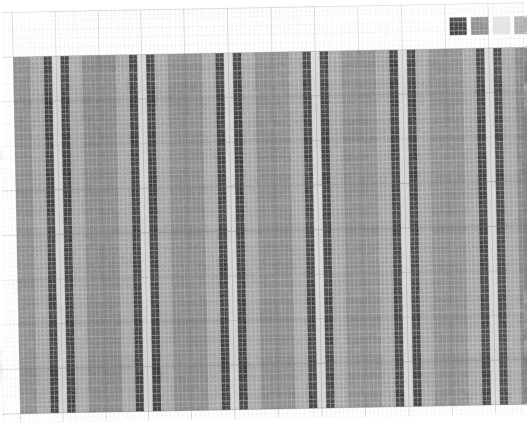

Rug
COLOURWAY 2

61 cm x 92 cm
(24 in. x 36 in.)

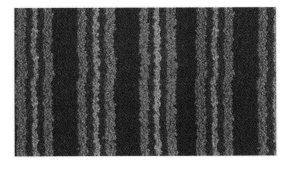

Shade	Code	Lengths	Packs
Sandalwood	(76)	1920	13
Loam Brown	(28)	3840	25
Light Sand	(87)	960	7
Tan	(32)	2880	19

▼ *61 cm x 92 cm*

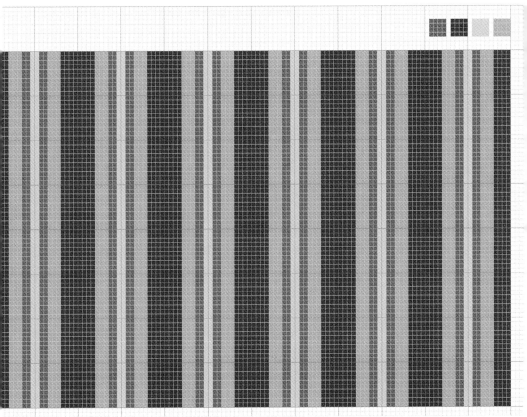

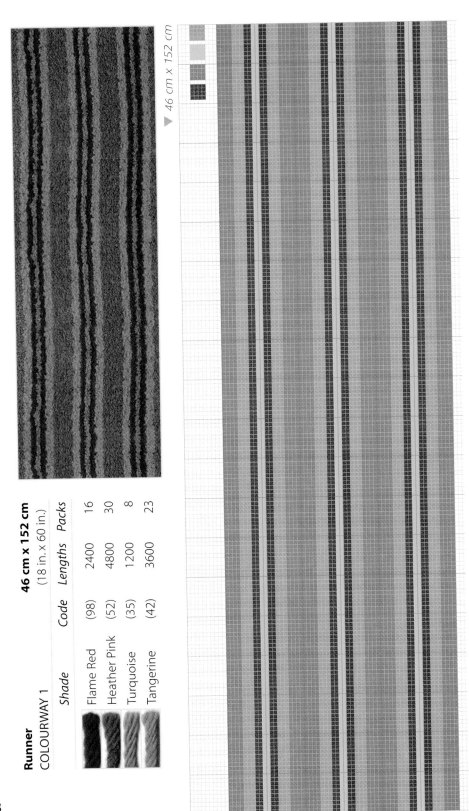

Runner
COLOURWAY 1

46 cm x 152 cm
(18 in. x 60 in.)

Shade	Code	Lengths	Packs
Flame Red	(98)	2400	16
Heather Pink	(52)	4800	30
Turquoise	(35)	1200	8
Tangerine	(42)	3600	23

46 cm x 152 cm

Runner
COLOURWAY 2

46 cm x 152 cm
(18 in. x 60 in.)

Shade	Code	Lengths	Packs
Sandalwood	(76)	2400	16
Loam Brown	(28)	4800	30
Light Sand	(87)	1200	8
Tan	(32)	3600	23

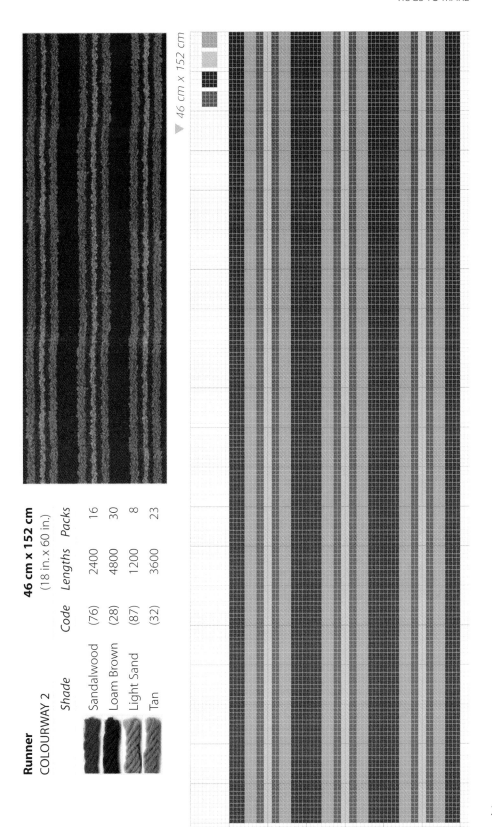

▼ 46 cm x 152 cm

stripe me down

FINISHED SIZE

- Rug: 61cm x 92cm (24 in. x 36 in.) made up from four individual sections each 30cm x 46cm (12 in. x 18 in.)
- Runner: 46cm x 152cm (18 in. x 60 in.) made up from five individual sections each 30cm x 46cm (12 in. x 18 in.).

YOU WILL NEED:

- Latch-hook
- Strong thread
- Sharp sewing needle
- Latch-hook canvas pieces for each individual section, 40 x 60 holes between selvedges, plus selvedge allowance
- 6.5cm (2½ in.) lengths of rug wool in the colours below (packs contain approximately 160 pieces).

INSTRUCTIONS

- To bind as you hook, fold under four-hole width at each raw edge. Bind the selvedges through the double canvas at each end as you work.
- Work in horizontal rows, following the chart carefully.
- Turn under and sew bound selvedges to the underside of the completed piece. Finish as desired.

Rug section COLOURWAY 1		30 cm x 46 cm (12 in. x 18 in.)		COLOURWAY 2	30 cm x 46 cm (12 in. x 18 in.)	
Shade	Code	Lengths	Packs	Shade		Code
Biscuit	(2)	120	1	Ice Blue		(12)
Indian Orange	(41)	120	1	Shell Pink		(72)
Flame Red	(98)	360	3	Heather Pink		(52)
Cardinal	(65)	360	3	Bluebird		(74)
Deep Coral	(93)	360	3	Lemon		(63)
Ruby	(60)	1080	7	Pale Green		(614)

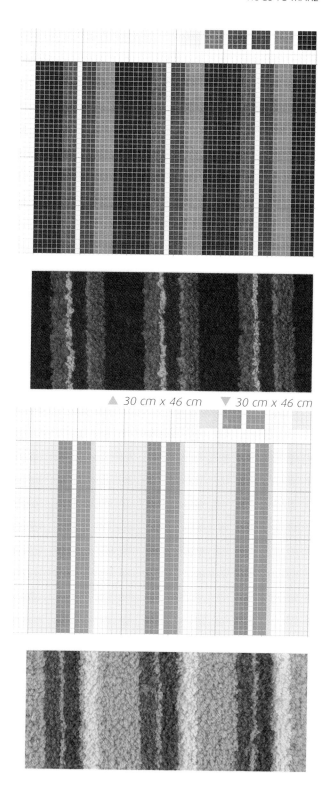

▲ 30 cm x 46 cm   ▼ 30 cm x 46 cm

Rug		**61 cm x 92 cm**	
COLOURWAY 1		(24 in. x 36 in.)	

	Shade	Code	Lengths	Packs
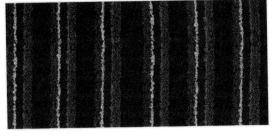	Biscuit	(2)	480	4
	Indian Orange	(41)	480	4
	Flame Red	(98)	1440	10
	Cardinal	(65)	1440	10
	Deep Coral	(93)	1440	10
	Ruby	(60)	4320	28

▼ *61 cm x 92 cr*

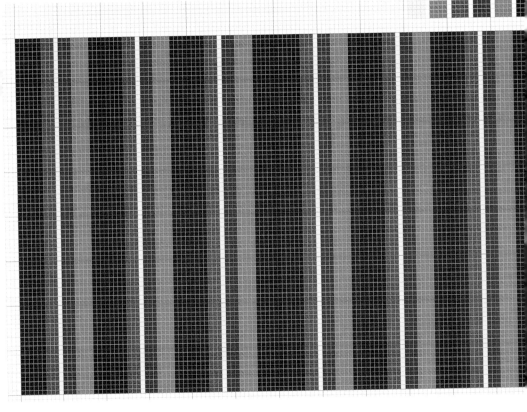

Rug   **61 cm x 92 cm**
COLOURWAY 2   (24 in. x 36 in.)

Shade		Code	Lengths	Packs
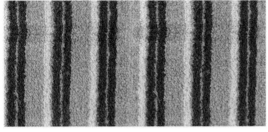	Ice Blue	(12)	480	4
	Shell Pink	(72)	480	4
	Heather Pink	(52)	1440	10
	Bluebird	(74)	1440	10
	Lemon	(63)	1440	10
	Pale Green	(614)	4320	28

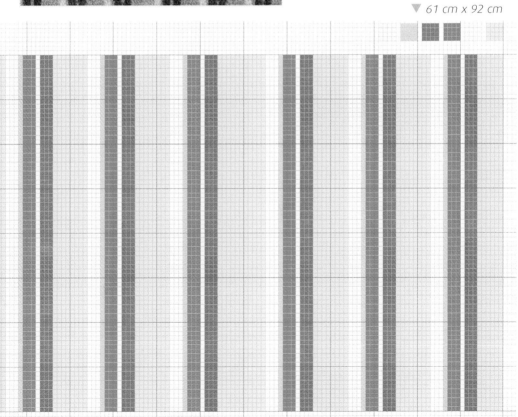

▼ *61 cm x 92 cm*

33

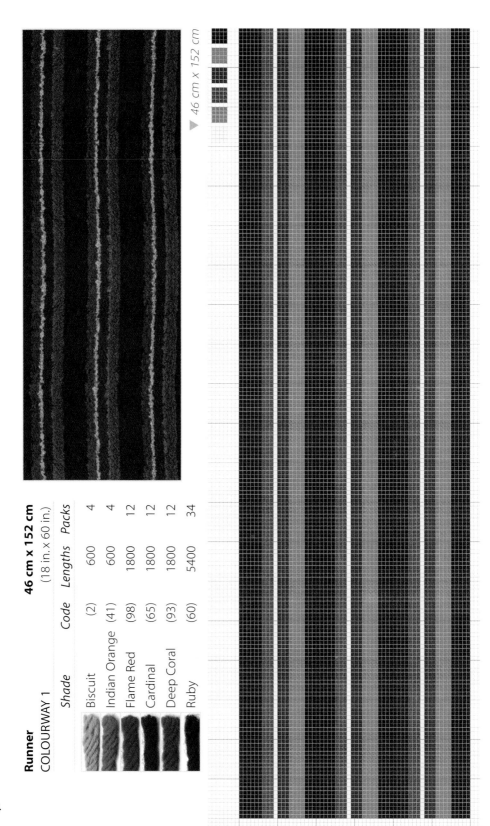

Runner
COLOURWAY 1

46 cm x 152 cm
(18 in. x 60 in.)

Shade	Code	Lengths	Packs
Biscuit	(2)	600	4
Indian Orange	(41)	600	4
Flame Red	(98)	1800	12
Cardinal	(65)	1800	12
Deep Coral	(93)	1800	12
Ruby	(60)	5400	34

46 cm x 152 cm

Runner
COLOURWAY 2

46 cm x 152 cm
(18 in. x 60 in.)

Shade	Code	Lengths	Packs
Ice Blue	(12)	600	4
Shell Pink	(72)	600	4
Heather Pink	(52)	1800	12
Bluebird	(74)	1800	12
Lemon	(63)	1800	12
Pale Green	(614)	5400	34

46 cm x 152 cm

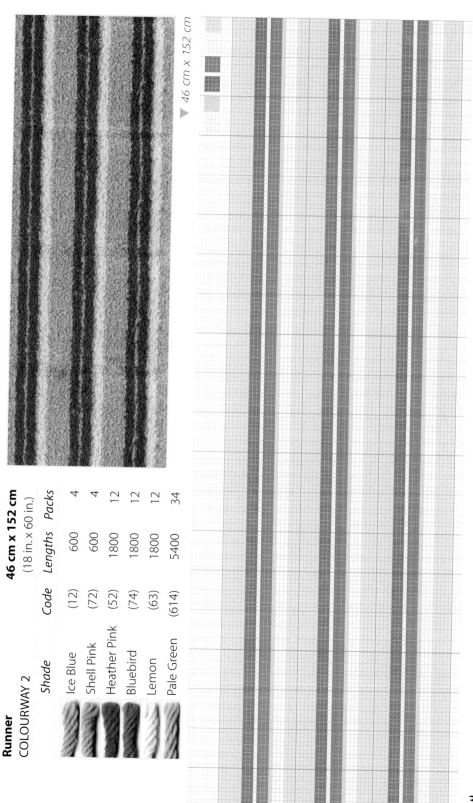

landing stripe

FINISHED SIZE
- Rug: 61cm x 92cm (24 in. x 36 in.) made up from four individual sections each 30cm x 46cm (12 in. x 18 in.)
- Runner: 46cm x 152cm (18 in. x 60 in.) made up from five individual sections each 30cm x 46cm (12 in. x 18 in.).

YOU WILL NEED:
- Latch-hook
- Strong thread
- Sharp sewing needle
- Latch-hook canvas pieces for each individual section, 40 x 60 holes between selvedges, plus selvedge allowance
- 6.5cm (2 ½ in.) lengths of rug wool in the colours below (packs contain approximately 160 pieces).

INSTRUCTIONS
- To bind as you hook, fold under four-hole width at each raw edge. Bind the selvedges through the double canvas at each end as you work.
- Work in horizontal rows, following the chart carefully.
- Turn under and sew bound selvedges to the underside of the completed piece. Finish as desired.

Rug section COLOURWAY 1		30 cm x 46 cm (12 in. x 18 in.)		COLOURWAY 2	30 cm x 46 cm (12 in. x 18 in.)	
	Shade	*Code*	*Lengths*	*Packs*	*Shade*	*Code*
	Cardinal	(65)	600	4	Jade Green	(7)
	Navy Blue	(37)	720	5	Spring Green	(17)
	Light Grey	(29)	480	4	Pale Green	(614)
	Old Gold	(88)	120	1	Evergreen	(22)
	Biscuit	(2)	480	4	Grass Green	(39)

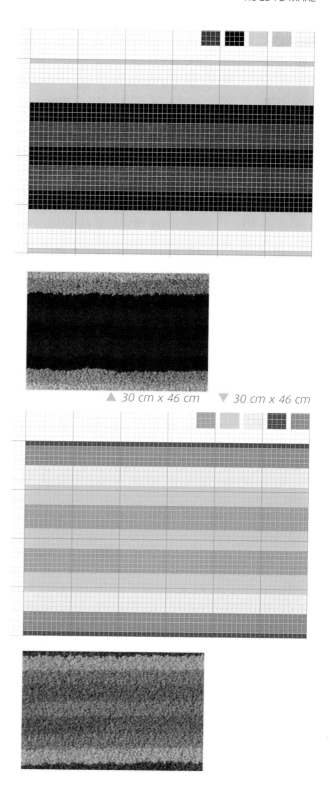

▲ 30 cm x 46 cm   ▼ 30 cm x 46 cm

| **Rug** | | **61 cm x 92 cm** | |
| COLOURWAY 1 | | (24 in. x 36 in.) | |

	Shade	Code	Lengths	Packs
	Cardinal	(65)	2400	16
	Navy Blue	(37)	2880	19
	Light Grey	(29)	1920	13
	Old Gold	(88)	480	4
	Biscuit	(2)	1920	13

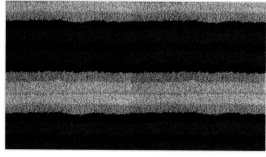

▼ 61 cm x 92

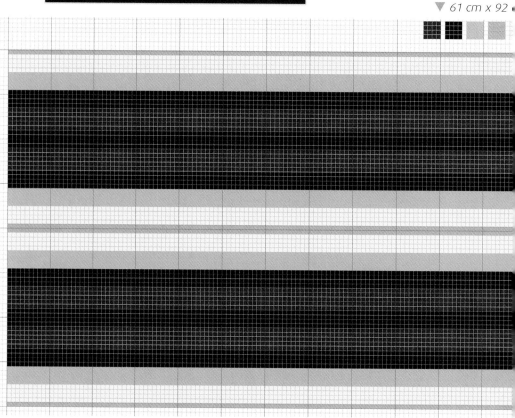

Rug
COLOURWAY 2

61 cm x 92 cm
(24 in. x 36 in.)

	Shade	Code	Lengths	Packs
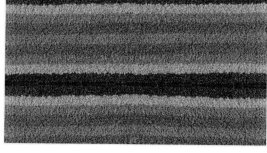	Jade Green	(7)	2400	16
	Spring Green	(17)	2880	19
	Pale Green	(614)	1920	13
	Evergreen	(22)	480	4
	Grass Green	(39)	1920	13

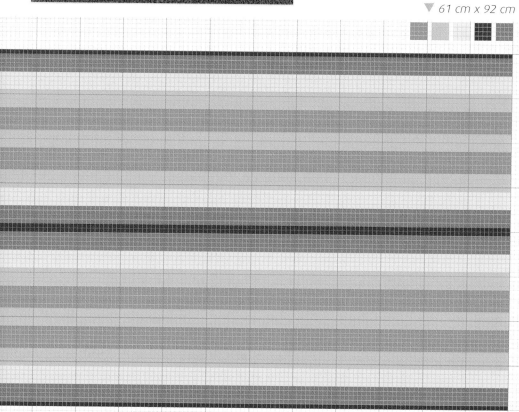

▼ *61 cm x 92 cm*

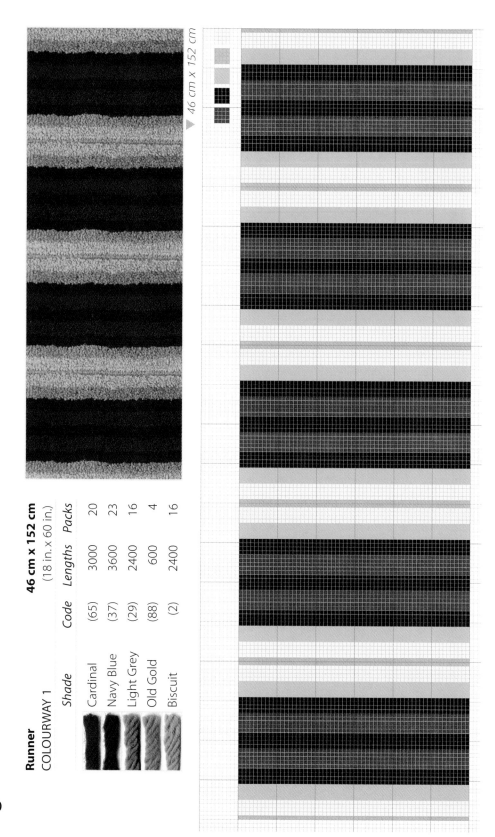

Runner
COLOURWAY 1

46 cm x 152 cm
(18 in. x 60 in.)

Shade	Code	Lengths	Packs
Cardinal	(65)	3000	20
Navy Blue	(37)	3600	23
Light Grey	(29)	2400	16
Old Gold	(88)	600	4
Biscuit	(2)	2400	16

46 cm x 152 cm

Runner
COLOURWAY 2

46 cm x 152 cm
(18 in. x 60 in.)

Shade	Code	Lengths	Packs
Jade Green	(7)	3000	20
Spring Green	(17)	3600	23
Pale Green	(614)	2400	16
Evergreen	(22)	600	4
Grass Green	(39)	2400	16

46 cm x 152 cm

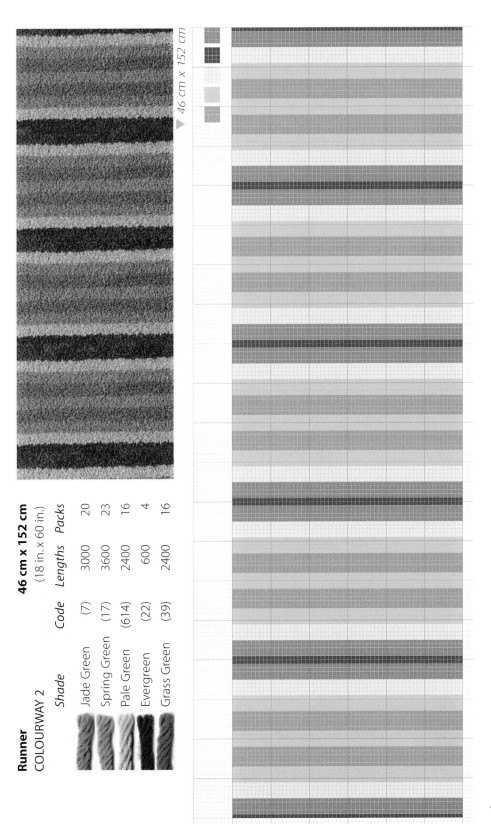

stripe hype

FINISHED SIZE
- Rug: 61cm x 92cm (24 in. x 36 in.) made up from four individual sections each 30cm x 46cm (12 in. x 18 in.)
- Runner: 46cm x 152cm (18 in. x 60 in.) made up from five individual sections each 30cm x 46cm (12 in. x 18 in.).

YOU WILL NEED:
- Latch-hook
- Strong thread
- Sharp sewing needle
- Latch-hook canvas pieces for each individual section, 40 x 60 holes between selvedges, plus selvedge allowance
- 6.5cm (2 ½ in.) lengths of rug wool in the colours below (packs contain approximately 160 pieces).

INSTRUCTIONS
- To bind as you hook, fold under four-hole width at each raw edge. Bind the selvedges through the double canvas at each end as you work.
- Work in horizontal rows, following the chart carefully.
- Turn under and sew bound selvedges to the underside of the completed piece. Finish as desired.

Rug section		30 cm x 46 cm			30 cm x 46 cm	
COLOURWAY 1		(12 in. x 18 in.)		COLOURWAY 2	(12 in. x 18 in.)	
Shade	*Code*	*Lengths*	*Packs*		*Shade*	*Code*
Hydrangea Blue	(23)	600	4		Heather Pink	(52)
Bluebird	(74)	240	2		Shell Pink	(72)
Ice Blue	(12)	1560	10		Pale Peach	(77)

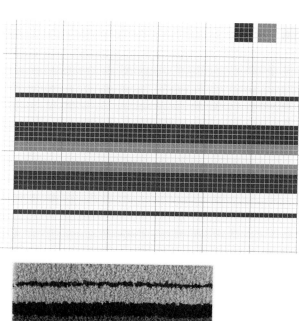

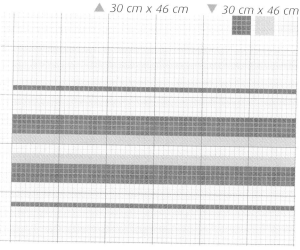

▲ 30 cm x 46 cm   ▼ 30 cm x 46 cm

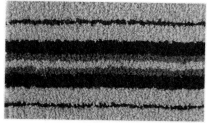

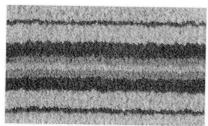

Rug   **61 cm x 92 cm**
COLOURWAY 1   (24 in. x 36 in.)

	Shade	Code	Lengths	Packs
	Hydrangea Blue	(23)	2400	16
	Bluebird	(74)	960	7
	Ice Blue	(12)	6240	40

▼ 61 cm x 92 cm

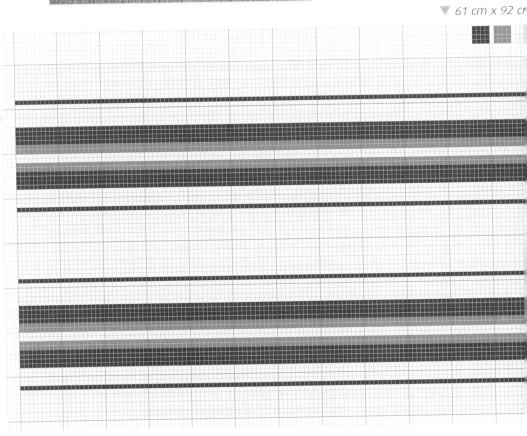

Rug **61 cm x 92 cm**
COLOURWAY 2 (24 in. x 36 in.)

Shade	Code	Lengths	Packs
Heather Pink	(52)	2400	16
Shell Pink	(72)	960	7
Pale Peach	(77)	6240	40

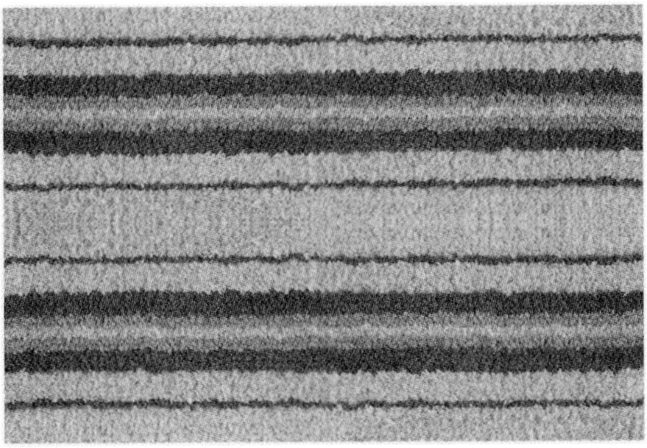

61 cm x 92 cm

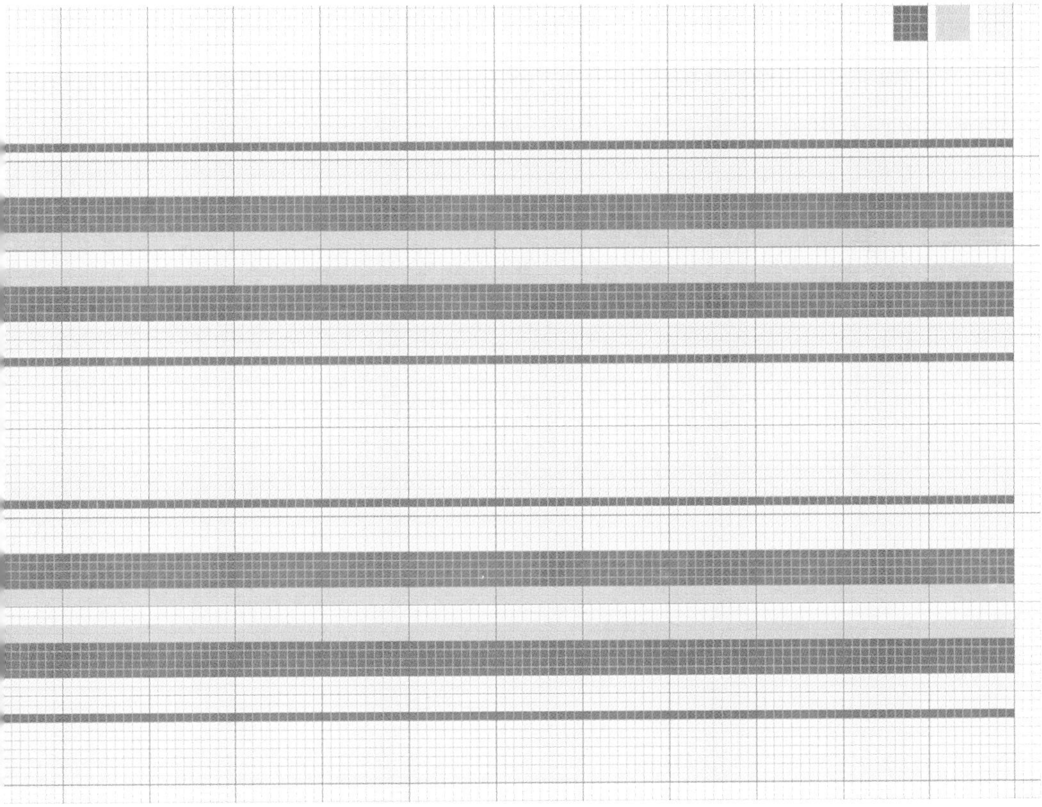

45

Runner
COLOURWAY 1

46 cm x 152 cm
(18 in. x 60 in.)

Shade	Code	Lengths	Packs
Hydrangea Blue	(23)	3000	20
Bluebird	(74)	1200	8
Ice Blue	(12)	7800	49

46 cm x 152 cm

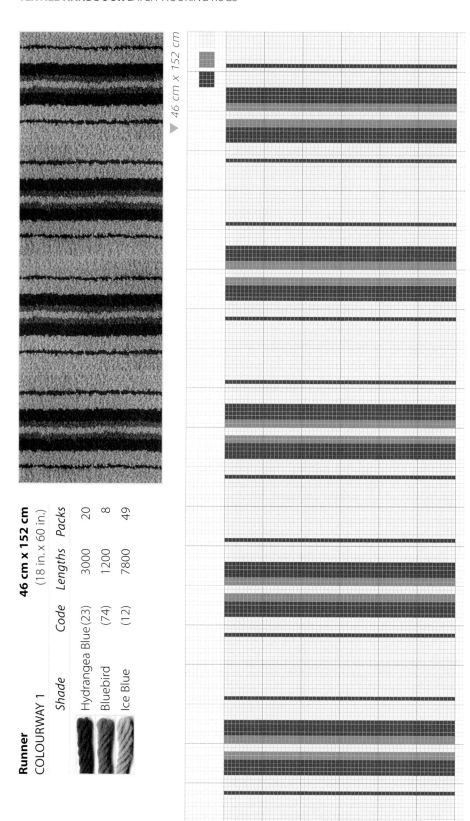

Runner **46 cm x 152 cm**
COLOURWAY 2 (18 in. x 60 in.)

Shade	Code	Lengths	Packs
Heather Pink	(52)	3000	20
Shell Pink	(72)	1200	8
Pale Peach	(77)	7800	49

46 cm x 152 cm

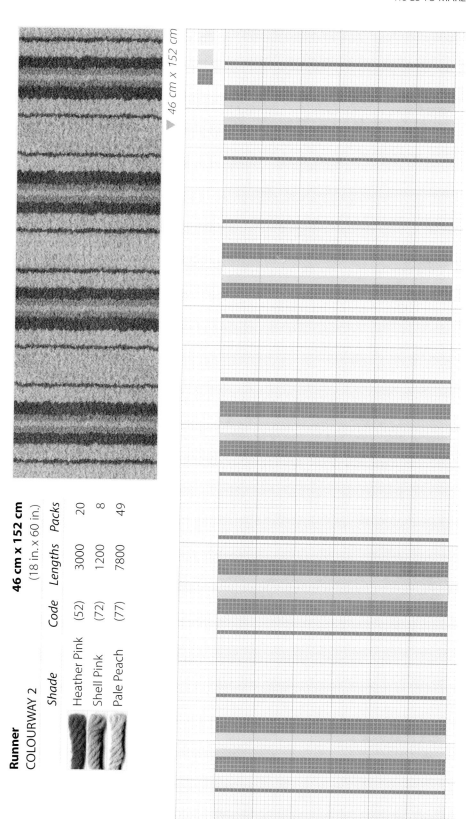

stripe hype mixed rug

■ 61cm x 92cm (24 in. x 36 in.)

	Shade	Code	Lengths	Packs
	Hydrangea Blue	(23)	1200	8
	Bluebird	(74)	480	4
	Ice Blue	(12)	3120	20
	Heather Pink	(52)	1200	8
	Shell Pink	(72)	480	4
	Pale Peach	(77)	3120	20

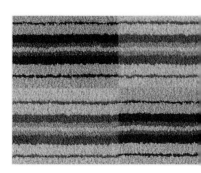

▼ 61 cm x 92 c

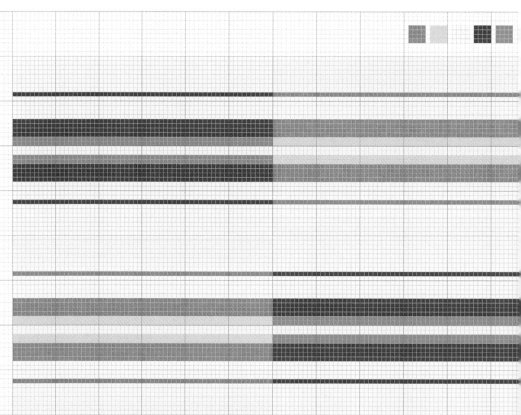

stripe hype mixed runner

■ 46cm x 152cm (18 in. x 60 in.)

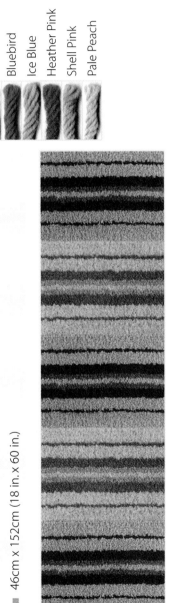

Shade	Code	Lengths	Packs
Hydrangea Blue	(23)	1800	12
Bluebird	(74)	720	5
Ice Blue	(12)	4680	30
Heather Pink	(52)	1200	8
Shell Pink	(72)	480	4
Pale Peach	(77)	3120	20

▼ 46 cm x 152 cm

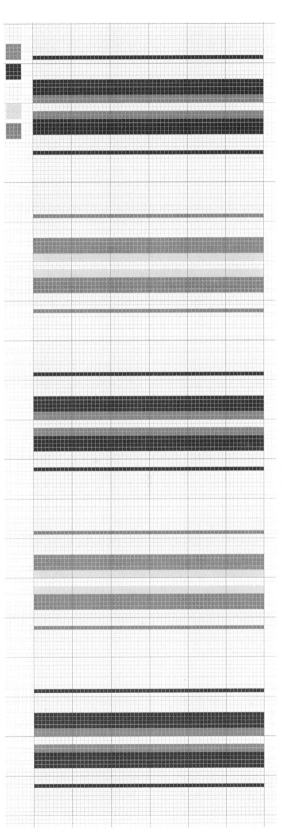

Cheeky Checks

When you repeat squares or lines they will become checks or striped patterns or a combination of the two. Checks are a great way of introducing lots of different colours into a room – experiment to find your favourite combinations.

cross check

FINISHED SIZE
- Rug: 61 cm x 92 cm (24 in. x 36 in.) made up from six individual sections each 30 cm x 30 cm (12 in. x 12 in.)

YOU WILL NEED:
- Latch-hook
- Strong thread
- Sharp sewing needle
- Latch-hook canvas pieces for each individual section, 40 x 40 holes between selvedges, plus selvedge allowance
- 6.5cm (2 ½ in.) lengths of rug wool in the colours below (packs contain approximately 160 pieces). I have multiplied this recipe by six to make it easier for you if you want to make the complete rug as charted.

INSTRUCTIONS
- To bind as you hook, fold under four-hole width at each raw edge. Bind the selvedges through the double canvas at each end as you work.
- Work in horizontal rows, following the chart carefully.
- Turn under and sew bound selvedges to the underside of the completed piece. Finish as desired.

Shade	Code	30 cm x 30 cm (12 in. x 12 in.) Lengths	Packs	61 cm x 92 cm (24 in. x 36 in.) Lengths	Packs
Biscuit	(2)	111	1	666	5
Old Gold	(88)	102	1	612	4
Dark Amber	(3)	170	2	1020	7
Tobacco Brown	(26)	74	1	444	3
Turquoise	(35)	96	1	576	4
Aqua	(45)	210	2	1260	8
Teal Blue	(25)	837	6	5022	32

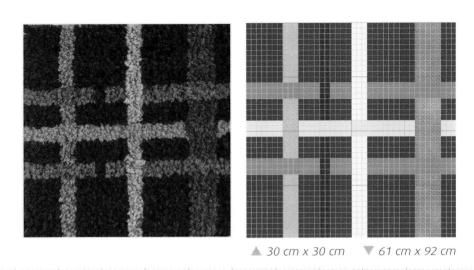

▲ 30 cm x 30 cm ▼ 61 cm x 92 cm

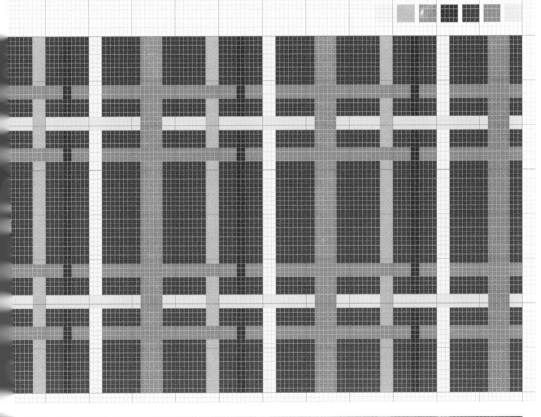

check point

FINISHED SIZE

■ Rug: 61 cm x 92 cm (24 in. x 36 in.) made up from six individual sections each 30 cm x 30 cm (12 in. x 12 in.)

YOU WILL NEED:

■ Latch-hook
■ Strong thread
■ Sharp sewing needle
■ Latch-hook canvas pieces for each individual section, 40 x 40 holes between selvedges, plus selvedge allowance
■ 6.5cm (2 ½ in.) lengths of rug wool in the colours below (packs contain approximately 160 pieces). I have multiplied this recipe by six to make it easier for you if you want to make the complete rug as charted.

INSTRUCTIONS

■ To bind as you hook, fold under four-hole width at each raw edge. Bind the selvedges through the double canvas at each end as you work.
■ Work in horizontal rows, following the chart carefully.
■ Turn under and sew bound selvedges to the underside of the completed piece. Finish as desired.

	Shade	Code	30 cm x 30 cm (12 in. x 12 in.)		61 cm x 92 cm (24 in. x 36 in.)	
			Lengths	Packs	Lengths	Packs
	Deep Coral	(93)	240	2	1440	10
	Bluebird	(74)	240	2	1440	10
	Light Grey	(29)	240	2	1440	10
	Grass Green	(39)	240	2	1440	10
	Biscuit	(2)	240	2	1440	10
	Black	(48)	400	3	2400	16

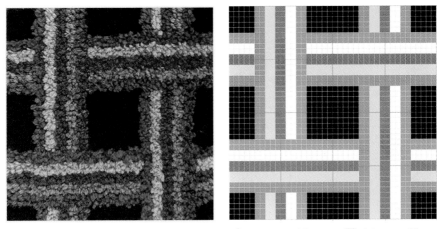

▲ 30 cm x 30 cm ▼ 61 cm x 92 cm

check your speed

FINISHED SIZE

- Rug: 61 cm x 92 cm (24 in. x 36 in.) made up from six individual sections each 30 cm x 30 cm (12 in. x 12 in.)

YOU WILL NEED:

- Latch-hook
- Strong thread
- Sharp sewing needle
- Latch-hook canvas pieces for each individual section, 40 x 40 holes between selvedges, plus selvedge allowance
- 6.5cm (2 ½ in.) lengths of rug wool in the colours below (packs contain approximately 160 pieces). I have multiplied this recipe by six to make it easier for you if you want to make the complete rug as charted.

INSTRUCTIONS

- To bind as you hook, fold under four-hole width at each raw edge. Bind the selvedges through the double canvas at each end as you work.
- Work in horizontal rows, following the chart carefully.
- Turn under and sew bound selvedges to the underside of the completed piece. Finish as desired.

COLOURWAY 1			30 cm x 30 cm (12 in. x 12 in.)		61 cm x 92 cm (24 in. x 36 in.)	
Shade	Code	Lengths	Packs		Lengths	Packs
White	(36)	400	3		2400	16
Lavender	(61)	160	2		960	7
Iris Purple	(54)	160	2		960	7
Spanish Yellow	(31)	80	1		480	4
Flame Red	(98)	160	2		960	7
Black	(48)	320	3		1920	13
Heather Pink	(52)	160	2		960	7
Emerald Green	(97)	160	2		960	7

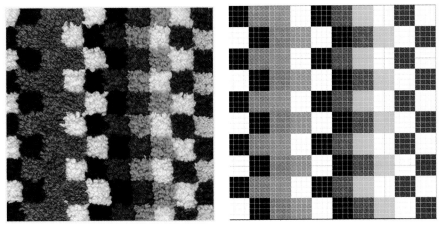

▲ 30 cm x 30 cm   ▼ 61 cm x 92 cm

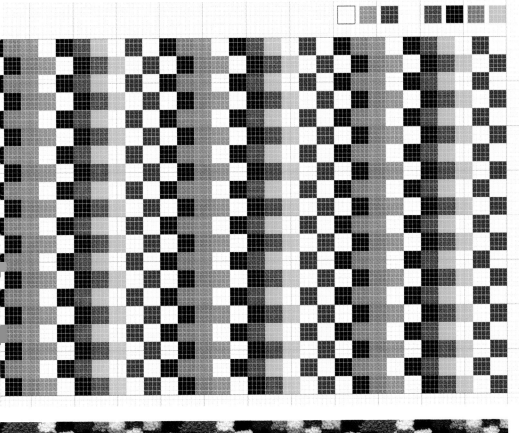

COLOURWAY 2			30 cm x 30 cm (12 in. x 12 in.)		61 cm x 92 cm (24 in. x 36 in.)	
Shade	Code		Lengths	Packs	Lengths	Packs
Grass Green	(39)		400	3	2400	16
Tobacco Brown	(26)		160	2	960	7
Loam Brown	(28)		160	2	960	7
Pale Green	(614)		80	1	480	4
Mid Turquoise	(19)		160	2	960	7
Bright Orange	(1)		320	3	1920	13
Deep Coral	(93)		160	2	960	7
Biscuit	(2)		160	2	960	7

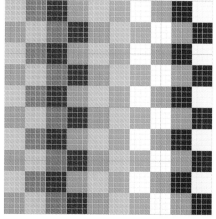

▲ *30 cm x 30 cm*

▲ 61 cm x 92 cm

check mate

FINISHED SIZE
■ Rug: 61 cm x 92 cm (24 in. x 36 in.) made up from six individual sections each 30 cm x 30 cm (12 in. x 12 in.)

YOU WILL NEED:
■ Latch-hook
■ Strong thread
■ Sharp sewing needle
■ Latch-hook canvas pieces for each individual section, 40 x 40 holes between selvedges, plus selvedge allowance
■ 6.5cm (2 ½ in.) lengths of rug wool in the colours below (packs contain approximately 160 pieces). I have multiplied this recipe by six to make it easier for you if you want to make the complete rug as charted.

INSTRUCTIONS
■ To bind as you hook, fold under four-hole width at each raw edge. Bind the selvedges through the double canvas at each end as you work.
■ Work in horizontal rows, following the chart carefully.
■ Turn under and sew bound selvedges to the underside of the completed piece. Finish as desired.

Shade	Code	30 cm x 30 cm (12 in. x 12 in.) Lengths	Packs	61 cm x 92 cm (24 in. x 36 in.) Lengths	Packs
Ice Blue	(12)	272	3	1632	11
Pale Green	(614)	365	3	2190	14
Oriental Gold	(44)	559	4	3354	21
Black	(48)	80	1	480	3
Flame Red	(98)	68	1	408	3
Hydrangea Blue	(23)	256	2	1536	10

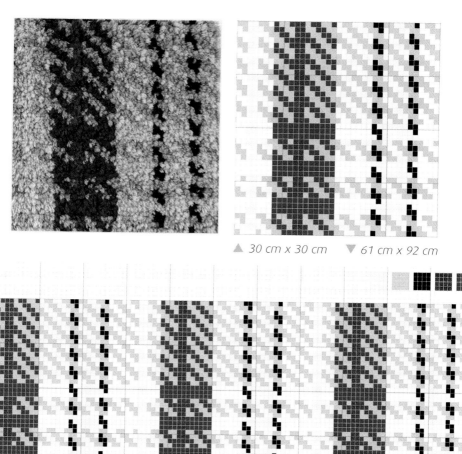

▲ 30 cm x 30 cm   ▼ 61 cm x 92 cm

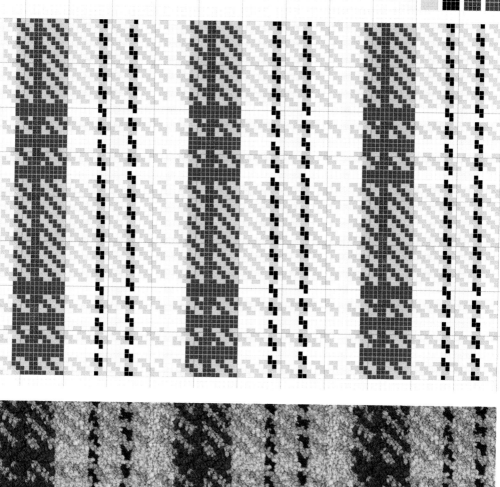

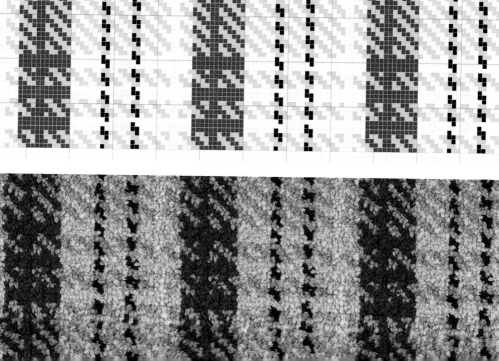

Cheeky Checks rugs

BUILDING BLOCKS

You can overlap these blocks, push them around a bit or even omit whole sections to create different shapes and contrasts. Irregular shapes will soon appear from regular shapes with a bit of manipulation and coaxing.

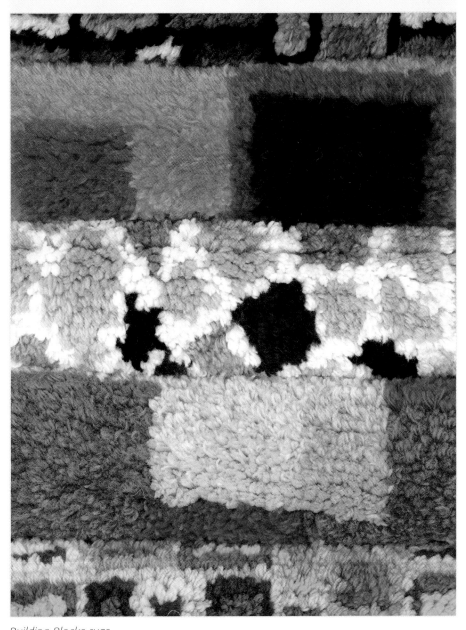

Building Blocks rugs

metropolis

I have created two colourways for this design to conjure up visions of New York at night and New York in the day. It just depends which background you choose – are you a night-owl or an early riser?

FINISHED SIZE
■ Rug: 61 cm x 92 cm (24 in. x 36 in.) made up from six individual sections each 30 cm x 30 cm (12 in. x 12 in.)

YOU WILL NEED:
■ Latch-hook
■ Strong thread
■ Sharp sewing needle
■ Latch-hook canvas pieces for each individual section, 40 x 40 holes between selvedges, plus selvedge allowance
■ 6.5cm (2 ½ in.) lengths of rug wool in the colours below (packs contain approximately 160 pieces). I have multiplied this recipe by six to make it easier for you if you want to make the complete rug as charted.

INSTRUCTIONS
■ To bind as you hook, fold under four-hole width at each raw edge. Bind the selvedges through the double canvas at each end as you work.
■ Work in horizontal rows, following the chart carefully.
■ Turn under and sew bound selvedges to the underside of the completed piece. Finish as desired.

COLOURWAY 1			30 cm x 30 cm (12 in. x 12 in.)		61 cm x 92 cm (24 in. x 36 in.)	
	Shade	Code	Lengths	Packs	Lengths	Packs
	Lavender	(61)	236	2	1416	9
	Bluebird	(74)	138	1	828	6
	Spanish Yellow	(31)	232	2	1392	9
	Tangerine	(42)	144	1	864	6
	Flame Red	(98)	249	2	1494	10
	Biscuit	(2)	435	3	2610	17
	Emerald Green	(97	)166	2	996	7

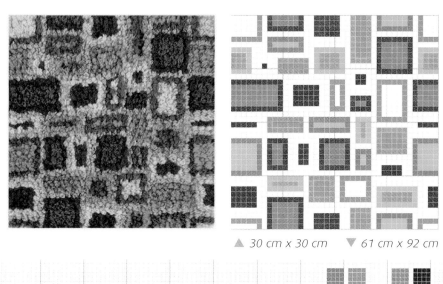

▲ 30 cm x 30 cm   ▼ 61 cm x 92 cm

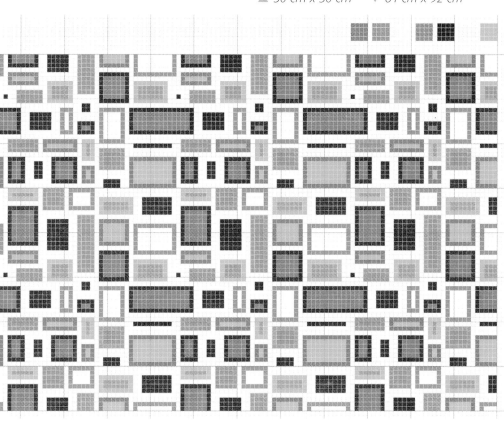

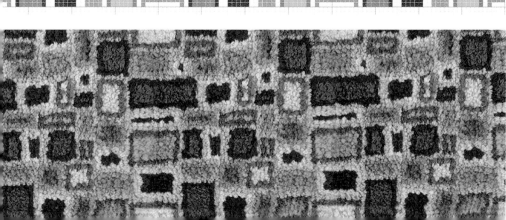

COLOURWAY 2			30 cm x 30 cm (12 in. x 12 in.)		61 cm x 92 cm (24 in. x 36 in.)	
Shade	Code	Lengths	Packs	Lengths	Packs
Lavender	(61)	236	2	1416	9
Bluebird	(74)	138	1	828	6
Spanish Yellow	(31)	232	2	1392	9
Tangerine	(42)	144	1	864	6
Flame Red	(98)	249	2	1494	10
Black	(48)	435	3	2610	17
Emerald Green	(97)	166	2	996	7

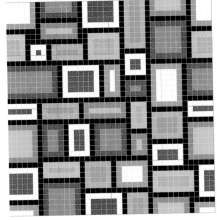

▲ *30 cm x 30 cm*

▲ 61 cm x 92 cm

sunset boulevard

Being very high up and watching the streams of traffic passing (guess where) brought this rug into being.

FINISHED SIZE

- Rug: 61 cm x 92 cm (24 in. x 36 in.) made up from six individual sections each 30 cm x 30 cm (12 in. x 12 in.)

YOU WILL NEED:

- Latch-hook
- Strong thread
- Sharp sewing needle
- Latch-hook canvas pieces for each individual section, 40 x 40 holes between selvedges, plus selvedge allowance
- 6.5cm (2 ½ in.) lengths of rug wool in the colours below (packs contain approximately 160 pieces). I have multiplied this recipe by six to make it easier for you if you want to make the complete rug as charted.

INSTRUCTIONS

- To bind as you hook, fold under four-hole width at each raw edge. Bind the selvedges through the double canvas at each end as you work.
- Work in horizontal rows, following the chart carefully.
- Turn under and sew bound selvedges to the underside of the completed piece. Finish as desired.

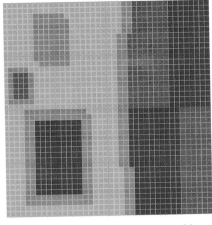

▲ *30 cm x 30 cm*

			30 cm x 30 cm (12 in. x 12 in.)		**61 cm x 92 cm** (24 in. x 36 in.)	
	Shade	*Code*	*Lengths*	*Packs*	*Lengths*	*Packs*
	Indian Orange	(41)	274	2	1644	11
	Flame Red	(98)	289	2	1734	11
	Cardinal	(65)	477	3	2862	18
	Tangerine	(42)	560	4	3360	22

▼ *61 cm x 92 cm*

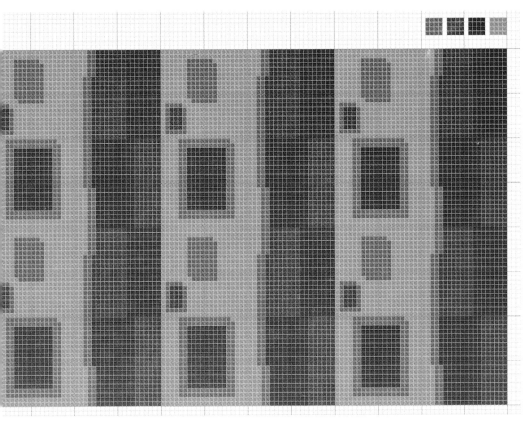

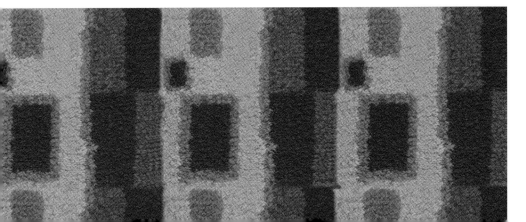

gridlock

So many traffic jams in cities all over the world causing such chaos… but cities are still such vibrant and exciting places.

FINISHED SIZE

- Rug: 61 cm x 92 cm (24 in. x 36 in.) made up from six individual sections each 30 cm x 30 cm (12 in. x 12 in.)

YOU WILL NEED:

- Latch-hook
- Strong thread
- Sharp sewing needle
- Latch-hook canvas pieces for each individual section, 40 x 40 holes between selvedges, plus selvedge allowance
- 6.5cm (2 ½ in.) lengths of rug wool in the colours below (packs contain approximately 160 pieces). I have multiplied this recipe by six to make it easier for you if you want to make the complete rug as charted.

INSTRUCTIONS

- To bind as you hook, fold under four-hole width at each raw edge. Bind the selvedges through the double canvas at each end as you work.
- Work in horizontal rows, following the chart carefully.
- Turn under and sew bound selvedges to the underside of the completed piece. Finish as desired.

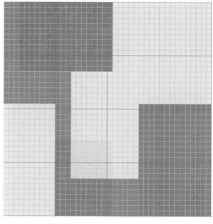

▲ *30 cm x 30 cm*

Shade	Code	30 cm x 30 cm (12 in. x 12 in.)		61 cm x 92 cm (24 in. x 36 in.)	
		Lengths	Packs	Lengths	Packs
Bluebird	(74)	173	2	1038	7
Shell Pink	(72)	56	1	336	3
Pale Green	(614)	745	5	4470	28
Heather Pink	(52)	626	4	3756	24

▼ *61 cm x 92 cm*

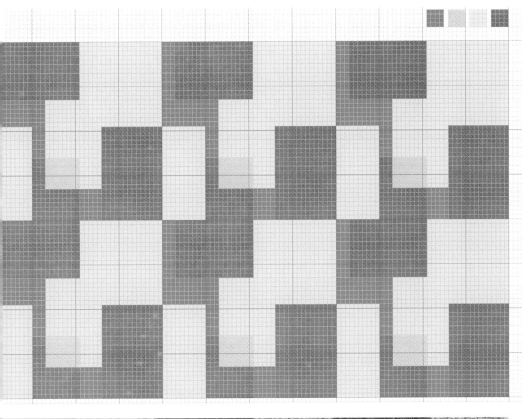

mosaic mania

My mum took a fantastic photo of a mosaic column on her intrepid travels. She thought that it would make a great rug and I think that she's right.

FINISHED SIZE
- Rug: 61 cm x 92 cm (24 in. x 36 in.) made up from six individual sections each 30 cm x 30 cm (12 in. x 12 in.)

YOU WILL NEED:
- Latch-hook
- Strong thread
- Sharp sewing needle
- Latch-hook canvas pieces for each individual section, 40 x 40 holes between selvedges, plus selvedge allowance
- 6.5cm (2 ½ in.) lengths of rug wool in the colours below (packs contain approximately 160 pieces). I have multiplied this recipe by six to make it easier for you if you want to make the complete rug as charted.

INSTRUCTIONS
- To bind as you hook, fold under four-hole width at each raw edge. Bind the selvedges through the double canvas at each end as you work.
- Work in horizontal rows, following the chart carefully.
- Turn under and sew bound selvedges to the underside of the completed piece. Finish as desired.

COLOURWAY 1			30 cm x 30 cm (12 in. x 12 in.)		61 cm x 92 cm (24 in. x 36 in.)	
	Shade	*Code*	*Lengths*	*Packs*	*Lengths*	*Packs*
	Light Grey	(29)	147	1	882	6
	Tobacco Brown	(26)	150	1	900	6
	Black	(48)	158	1	948	6
	Cream	(38)	554	4	3324	21
	Biscuit	(2)	591	4	3546	23

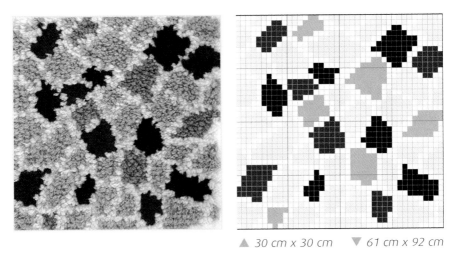

▲ 30 cm x 30 cm   ▼ 61 cm x 92 cm

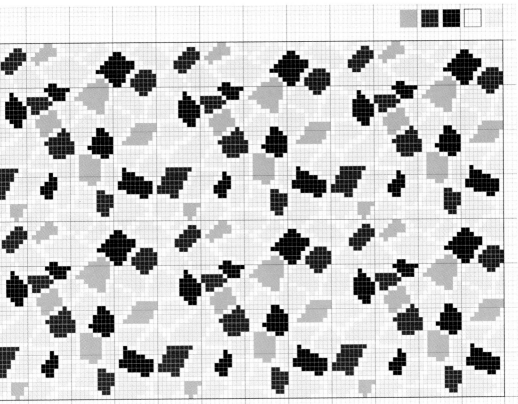

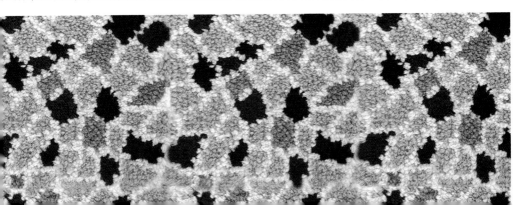

GROUNDWORK

Most of these designs have evolved from different ground, floor and wall surfaces and decorations that have caught my eye in various locations – I hope you enjoy making them into rugs.

Groundwork rugs

sidestep

I am always so worried that if I don't look down at the pavement whilst I am walking around that I might tread on something undesirable. What I have noticed is that the colours of the pavement look very different depending on the weather. So I have done two colourways for this design – the first depicting the pavement on a hot and sunny day and the second depicting that same stretch of pavement on a wet and cold day.

FINISHED SIZE
- Rug: 61 cm x 92 cm (24 in. x 36 in.) made up from six individual sections each 30 cm x 30 cm (12 in. x 12 in.)

YOU WILL NEED:
- Latch-hook
- Strong thread
- Sharp sewing needle
- Latch-hook canvas pieces for each individual section, 40 x 40 holes between selvedges, plus selvedge allowance
- 6.5cm (2 ½ in.) lengths of rug wool in the colours below (packs contain approximately 160 pieces). I have multiplied this recipe by six to make it easier for you if you want to make the complete rug as charted.

INSTRUCTIONS
- To bind as you hook, fold under four-hole width at each raw edge. Bind the selvedges through the double canvas at each end as you work.
- Work in horizontal rows, following the chart carefully.
- Turn under and sew bound selvedges to the underside of the completed piece. Finish as desired.

COLOURWAY 1			30 cm x 30 cm (12 in. x 12 in.)		61 cm x 92 cm (24 in. x 36 in.)	
Shade	Code	Lengths	Packs		Lengths	Packs
Shell Pink	(72)	120	1		720	5
Deep Coral	(93)	120	1		720	5
Lavender	(61)	120	1		720	5
Bluebird	(74)	240	2		1440	10
Spring Green	(17)	160	2		720	5
Spanish Yellow	(31)	160	2		720	5
Cream	(38)	360	3		2160	14
Oriental Gold	(44)	40	1		240	2
Light Green	(614)	80	1		480	4
Ice Blue	(12)	200	2		1200	8

▲ *30 cm x 30 cm*

▲ 61 cm x 92 cm

COLOURWAY 2		30 cm x 30 cm (12 in. x 12 in.)		61 cm x 92 cm (24 in. x 36 in.)	
Shade	Code	Lengths	Packs	Lengths	Packs
Indian Orange	(41)	120	1	720	5
Flame Red	(98)	120	1	720	5
Tangerine	(42)	120	1	720	5
Tobacco Brown	(26)	240	2	1440	10
Old Gold	(88)	160	2	720	5
Silver	(16)	160	2	720	5
Black	(48)	360	3	2160	14
White	(36)	40	1	480	4
Dark Amber	(3)	80	1	480	4
Biscuit	(2)	200	2	1200	8

▲ *30 cm x 30 cm*

▲ 61 cm x 92 cm

surface tension

Railroad tracks and tramlines were the leaping off point for this design.

FINISHED SIZE

- Rug: 61 cm x 92 cm (24 in. x 36 in.) made up from six individual sections each 30 cm x 30 cm (12 in. x 12 in.)

YOU WILL NEED:

- Latch-hook
- Strong thread
- Sharp sewing needle
- Latch-hook canvas pieces for each individual section, 40 x 40 holes between selvedges, plus selvedge allowance
- 6.5cm (2 ½ in.) lengths of rug wool in the colours below (packs contain approximately 160 pieces). I have multiplied this recipe by six to make it easier for you if you want to make the complete rug as charted.

INSTRUCTIONS

- To bind as you hook, fold under four-hole width at each raw edge. Bind the selvedges through the double canvas at each end as you work.
- Work in horizontal rows, following the chart carefully.
- Turn under and sew bound selvedges to the underside of the completed piece. Finish as desired.

Shade	Code	30 cm x 30 cm (12 in. x 12 in.)		61 cm x 92 cm (24 in. x 36 in.)	
		Lengths	Packs	Lengths	Packs
Indian Orange	(41)	192	2	1152	8
Hydrangea Blue	(23)	192	2	1152	8
Mid Turquoise	(19)	192	2	1152	8
Grass Green	(39)	192	2	1152	8
Biscuit	(2)	832	6	1152	8

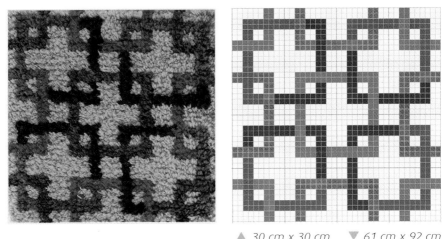

▲ 30 cm x 30 cm   ▼ 61 cm x 92 cm

retro route

I did a lot of groundwork for this book whilst sitting in the kitchen, at my computer, drinking very strong cups of coffee and staring at the walls for inspiration. After numerous cups of coffee and plenty of staring (I mean, thinking…) – this design evolved from my wallpaper.

FINISHED SIZE
- Rug: 61 cm x 92 cm (24 in. x 36 in.) made up from six individual sections each 30 cm x 30 cm (12 in. x 12 in.)

YOU WILL NEED:
- Latch-hook
- Strong thread
- Sharp sewing needle
- Latch-hook canvas pieces for each individual section, 40 x 40 holes between selvedges, plus selvedge allowance
- 6.5cm (2 ½ in.) lengths of rug wool in the colours below (packs contain approximately 160 pieces). I have multiplied this recipe by six to make it easier for you if you want to make the complete rug as charted.

INSTRUCTIONS
- To bind as you hook, fold under four-hole width at each raw edge. Bind the selvedges through the double canvas at each end as you work.
- Work in horizontal rows, following the chart carefully.
- Turn under and sew bound selvedges to the underside of the completed piece. Finish as desired.

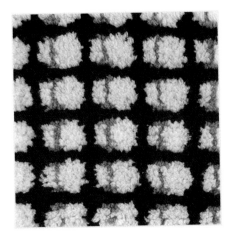
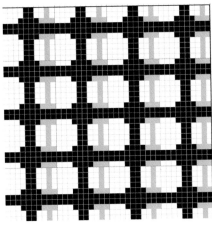

▲ *30 cm x 30 cm*

Shade	Code	30 cm x 30 cm (12 in. x 12 in.)		61 cm x 92 cm (24 in. x 36 in.)	
		Lengths	Packs	Lengths	Packs
White	(36)	720	5	4320	28
Light Grey	(29)	200	5	1200	8
Black	(48)	680	5	4080	26

▼ *61 cm x 92 cm*

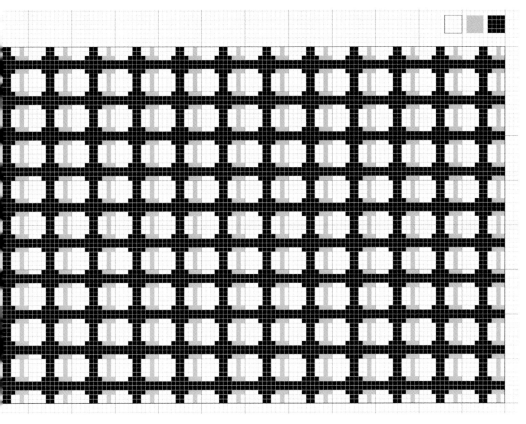

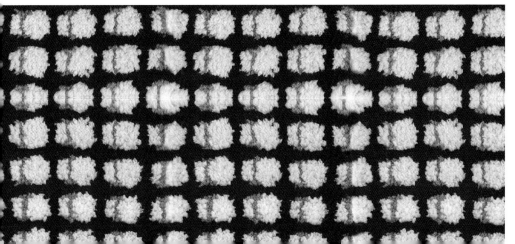

mind the gap

This design reminds me of the underground and trains and tunnels, and busy commuters neatly packed into any available space.

FINISHED SIZE

- Rug: 61 cm x 92 cm (24 in. x 36 in.) made up from six individual sections each 30 cm x 30 cm (12 in. x 12 in.)

YOU WILL NEED:

- Latch-hook
- Strong thread
- Sharp sewing needle
- Latch-hook canvas pieces for each individual section, 40 x 40 holes between selvedges, plus selvedge allowance
- 6.5cm (2 ½ in.) lengths of rug wool in the colours below (packs contain approximately 160 pieces). I have multiplied this recipe by six to make it easier for you if you want to make the complete rug as charted.

INSTRUCTIONS

- To bind as you hook, fold under four-hole width at each raw edge. Bind the selvedges through the double canvas at each end as you work.
- Work in horizontal rows, following the chart carefully.
- Turn under and sew bound selvedges to the underside of the completed piece. Finish as desired.

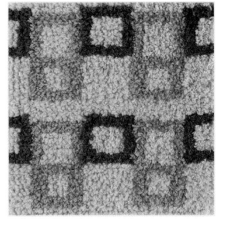 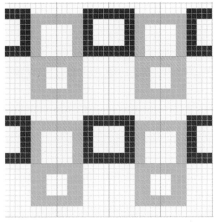

▲ *30 cm x 30 cm*

	Shade	Code	30 cm x 30 cm (12 in. x 12 in.)		61 cm x 92 cm (24 in. x 36 in.)	
			Lengths	Packs	Lengths	Packs
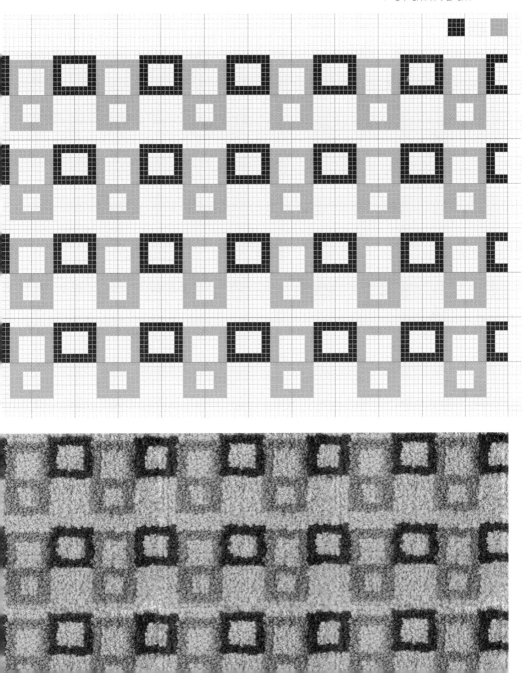	Iris Purple	(54)	240	2	1440	10
	Ice Blue	(12)	928	6	5568	35
	Oriental Gold	(44)	432	3	2592	17

▼ *61 cm x 92 cm*

SEE 3D

These pieces were designed to give the illusion of depth through clever use of colour. The effect is more striking when the shapes are filled with colour in strongly contrasting shades – you only have to look at the Stairway to Heaven variations (p.94) to see what I mean.

receding block

It's amazing what you can do with an old fashioned wooden matchstick or two.

FINISHED SIZE
- Rug: 61 cm x 92 cm (24 in. x 36 in.) made up from six individual sections each 30 cm x 30 cm (12 in. x 12 in.)

YOU WILL NEED:
- Latch-hook
- Strong thread
- Sharp sewing needle
- Latch-hook canvas pieces for each individual section, 40 x 40 holes between selvedges, plus selvedge allowance
- 6.5cm (2 ½ in.) lengths of rug wool in the colours below (packs contain approximately 160 pieces). I have multiplied this recipe by six to make it easier for you if you want to make the complete rug as charted.

INSTRUCTIONS
- To bind as you hook, fold under four-hole width at each raw edge. Bind the selvedges through the double canvas at each end as you work.
- Work in horizontal rows, following the chart carefully.
- Turn under and sew bound selvedges to the underside of the completed piece. Finish as desired.

Shade	Code	30 cm x 30 cm (12 in. x 12 in.)		61 cm x 92 cm (24 in. x 36 in.)	
		Lengths	*Packs*	*Lengths*	*Packs*
White	(36)	400	3	2400	16
Bluebird	(74)	400	3	2400	16
Indian Orange	(41)	400	3	2400	16
Black	(48)	400	3	2400	16

▲ 30 cm x 30 cm   ▼ 61 cm x 92 cm

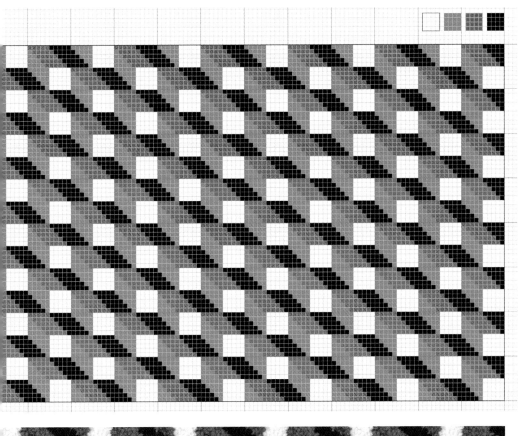

ribbons

Twisting and twirling ribbons are mesmerising – the longer the better.

FINISHED SIZE
- Rug: 61 cm x 92 cm (24 in. x 36 in.) made up from six individual sections each 30 cm x 30 cm (12 in. x 12 in.)

YOU WILL NEED:
- Latch-hook
- Strong thread
- Sharp sewing needle
- Latch-hook canvas pieces for each individual section, 40 x 40 holes between selvedges, plus selvedge allowance
- 6.5cm (2 ½ in.) lengths of rug wool in the colours below (packs contain approximately 160 pieces). I have multiplied this recipe by six to make it easier for you if you want to make the complete rug as charted.

INSTRUCTIONS
- To bind as you hook, fold under four-hole width at each raw edge. Bind the selvedges through the double canvas at each end as you work.
- Work in horizontal rows, following the chart carefully.
- Turn under and sew bound selvedges to the underside of the completed piece. Finish as desired.

▲ *30 cm x 30 cm*

Shade	Code	30 cm x 30 cm (12 in. x 12 in.)		61 cm x 92 cm (24 in. x 36 in.)	
		Lengths	Packs	Lengths	Packs
Cream	(38)	736	5	4416	28
Indian Orange	(41)	216	2	1296	9
Tangerine	(42)	216	2	1296	9
Evergreen	(22)	216	2	1296	9
Pale Green	(614)	216	2	1296	9

▼ 61 cm x 92 cm

stairway to heaven

This idea was conceived at a shopping mall. Whilst waiting around for a friend one day, I spent some time marvelling at the way an escalator goes up and comes down and seems to fold into nothing. Anyway there are two colourways and you can decide which is your up and which is your down escalator!

FINISHED SIZE

- Rug: 61 cm x 92 cm (24 in. x 36 in.) made up from six individual sections each 30 cm x 30 cm (12 in. x 12 in.)

YOU WILL NEED:

- Latch-hook
- Strong thread
- Sharp sewing needle
- Latch-hook canvas pieces for each individual section, 40 x 40 holes between selvedges, plus selvedge allowance
- 6.5cm (2 ½ in.) lengths of rug wool in the colours below (packs contain approximately 160 pieces). I have multiplied this recipe by six to make it easier for you if you want to make the complete rug as charted.

INSTRUCTIONS

- To bind as you hook, fold under four-hole width at each raw edge. Bind the selvedges through the double canvas at each end as you work.
- Work in horizontal rows, following the chart carefully.
- Turn under and sew bound selvedges to the underside of the completed piece. Finish as desired.

COLOURWAY 1			**30 cm x 30 cm** (12 in. x 12 in.)		**61 cm x 92 cm** (24 in. x 36 in.)	
Shade	*Code*	*Lengths*	*Packs*		*Lengths*	*Packs*
Bright Orange	(1)	400	3		2400	16
Biscuit	(2)	400	3		2400	16
Grass Green	(39)	400	3		2400	16
Mid Turquoise	(19)	400	3		2400	16

▲ 30 cm x 30 cm ▼ 61 cm x 92 cm

COLOURWAY 2			**30 cm x 30 cm** (12 in. x 12 in.)		**61 cm x 92 cm** (24 in. x 36 in.)	
	Shade	Code	Lengths	Packs	Lengths	Packs
	Pale Green	(614)	400	3	2400	16
	Bluebird	(74)	400	3	2400	16
	Tobacco Brown	(26)	400	3	2400	16
	Shell Pink	(72)	400	3	2400	16

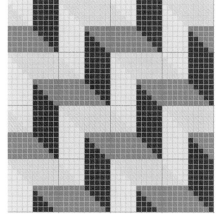

▲ *30 cm x 30 cm*

▲ *61 cm x 92 cm*

trellis

I like to spend as much time as possible in gardens, whether my own or those of friends, and there always seems to be a trellis somewhere nearby. This rug brings a little bit of the outdoors inside and will remind you of those wonderfully weighty summer colours during the greyer winter months.

FINISHED SIZE
- Rug: 61 cm x 92 cm (24 in. x 36 in.) made up from six individual sections each 30 cm x 30 cm (12 in. x 12 in.)

YOU WILL NEED:
- Latch-hook
- Strong thread
- Sharp sewing needle
- Latch-hook canvas pieces for each individual section, 40 x 40 holes between selvedges, plus selvedge allowance
- 6.5cm (2 ½ in.) lengths of rug wool in the colours below (packs contain approximately 160 pieces). I have multiplied this recipe by six to make it easier for you if you want to make the complete rug as charted.

INSTRUCTIONS
- To bind as you hook, fold under four-hole width at each raw edge. Bind the selvedges through the double canvas at each end as you work.
- Work in horizontal rows, following the chart carefully.
- Turn under and sew bound selvedges to the underside of the completed piece. Finish as desired.

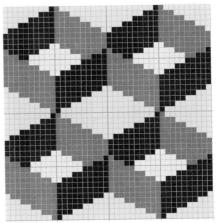

▲ *30 cm x 30 cm*

	Shade	Code	30 cm x 30 cm (12 in. x 12 in.)		61 cm x 92 cm (24 in. x 36 in.)	
			Lengths	Packs	Lengths	Packs
	Silver	(16)	144	1	864	6
	Heather Pink	(52)	528	4	3168	20
	Pale Green	(614)	400	3	2400	16
	Cardinal	(65)	520	4	3168	20

▼ *61 cm x 92 cm*

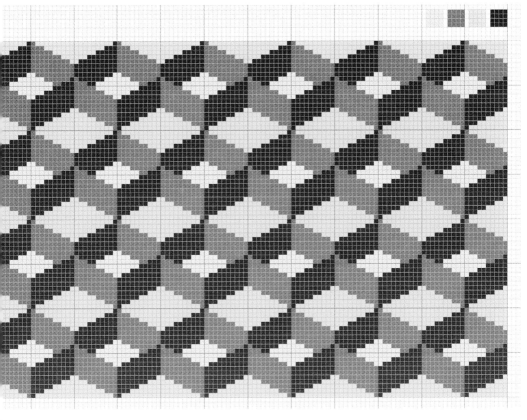

See 3D rugs

Bloomin' Gorgeous

One of the huge attractions of designing flower patterns is that they are so readily understood and enjoyed. I love flowers and am particularly fond of the ones that I have planted in my own garden; I love the bright colours and the excitement of not knowing which colour will be next to bloom. Flowers are a wonderful source of inspiration for me. The formal geometric pattern of Lazy Daisy has been hooked in repetitive colouring and looks very different from Soon To Bloom, the black and white flowers in Monochrome Magic. They are in fact exactly the same design. I hope you enjoy making your own carpets of flowers.

Bloomin' Gorgeous rugs

flourishing flowers

FINISHED SIZE
- Rug: 61 cm x 92 cm (24 in. x 36 in.) made up from six individual sections each 30 cm x 30 cm (12 in. x 12 in.)

YOU WILL NEED:
- Latch-hook
- Strong thread
- Sharp sewing needle
- Latch-hook canvas pieces for each individual section, 40 x 40 holes between selvedges, plus selvedge allowance
- 6.5cm (2 ½ in.) lengths of rug wool in the colours below (packs contain approximately 160 pieces). I have multiplied this recipe by six to make it easier for you if you want to make the complete rug as charted.

INSTRUCTIONS
- To bind as you hook, fold under four-hole width at each raw edge. Bind the selvedges through the double canvas at each end as you work.
- Work in horizontal rows, following the chart carefully.
- Turn under and sew bound selvedges to the underside of the completed piece. Finish as desired.

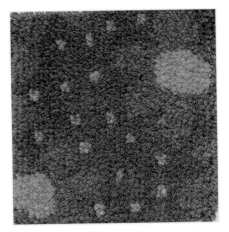 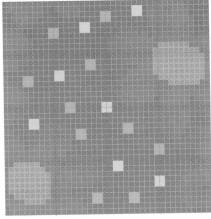

▲ *30 cm x 30 cm*

Shade		Code	30 cm x 30 cm (12 in. x 12 in.)		61 cm x 92 cm (24 in. x 36 in.)	
			Lengths	Packs	Lengths	Packs
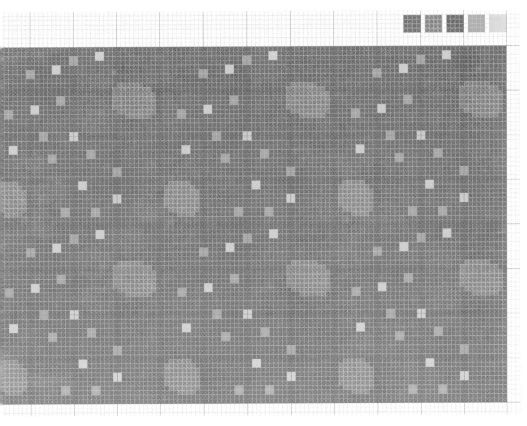 Lavender		(61)	773	5	4638	29
Tangerine		(42)	125	1	750	5
Heather Pink		(52)	634	4	3804	24
Emerald Green		(97)	40	1	240	2
Turquoise		(35)	28	1	168	2

▼ *61 cm x 92 cm*

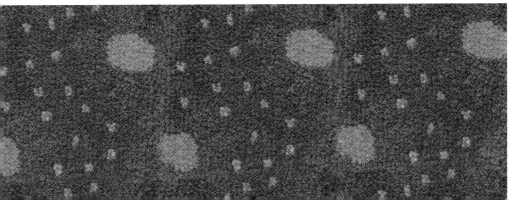

lazy daisy

Check out the black and white version, Soon to Bloom, with the
Monochrome Magic rugs on p.114.

FINISHED SIZE
- Rug: 61 cm x 92 cm (24 in. x 36 in.) made up from six individual sections
  each 30 cm x 30 cm (12 in. x 12 in.)

YOU WILL NEED:
- Latch-hook
- Strong thread
- Sharp sewing needle
- Latch-hook canvas pieces for each individual section, 40 x 40 holes
  between selvedges, plus selvedge allowance
- 6.5cm (2 ½ in.) lengths of rug wool in the colours below (packs contain
  approximately 160 pieces). I have multiplied this recipe by six to make it
  easier for you if you want to make the complete rug as charted.

INSTRUCTIONS
- To bind as you hook, fold under four-hole width at each raw edge. Bind
  the selvedges through the double canvas at each end as you work.
- Work in horizontal rows, following the chart carefully.
- Turn under and sew bound selvedges to the underside of the completed
  piece. Finish as desired.

Shade	Code	30 cm x 30 cm (12 in. x 12 in.)		61 cm x 92 cm (24 in. x 36 in.)	
		Lengths	Packs	Lengths	Packs
Aqua	(45)	160	2	960	7
Light Grey	(29)	800	6	4800	31
Dark Amber	(3)	160	2	960	7
Iris Purple	(54)	160	2	960	7
Old Gold	(88)	160	2	960	7
Cardinal	(65)	160	2	960	7

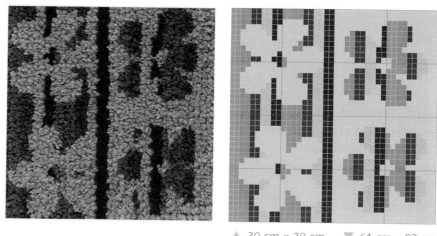

▲ 30 cm x 30 cm   ▼ 61 cm x 92 cm

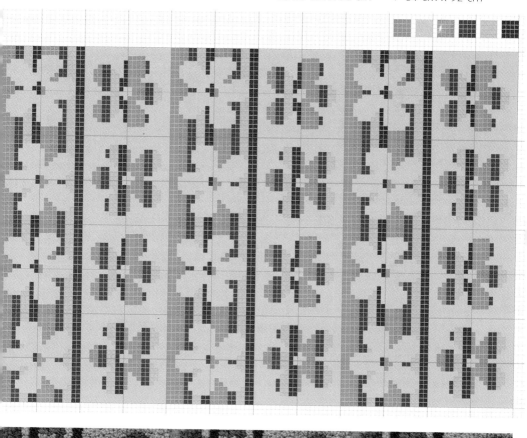

flower power

FINISHED SIZE
- Rug: 61 cm x 92 cm (24 in. x 36 in.) made up from six individual sections each 30 cm x 30 cm (12 in. x 12 in.)

YOU WILL NEED:
- Latch-hook
- Strong thread
- Sharp sewing needle
- Latch-hook canvas pieces for each individual section, 40 x 40 holes between selvedges, plus selvedge allowance
- 6.5cm (2 ½ in.) lengths of rug wool in the colours below (packs contain approximately 160 pieces). I have multiplied this recipe by six to make it easier for you if you want to make the complete rug as charted.

INSTRUCTIONS
- To bind as you hook, fold under four-hole width at each raw edge. Bind the selvedges through the double canvas at each end as you work.
- Work in horizontal rows, following the chart carefully.
- Turn under and sew bound selvedges to the underside of the completed piece. Finish as desired.

▲ *30 cm x 30 cm*

			30 cm x 30 cm (12 in. x 12 in.)		61 cm x 92 cm (24 in. x 36 in.)	
Shade	*Code*		*Lengths*	*Packs*	*Lengths*	*Packs*
White	(36)		260	2	1560	10
Flame Red	(98)		478	3	2868	18
Stewart Blue	(10)		297	2	1782	12
Spanish Yellow	(31)		230	2	1380	9
Black	(48)		335	3	2010	13

▼ *61 cm x 92 cm*

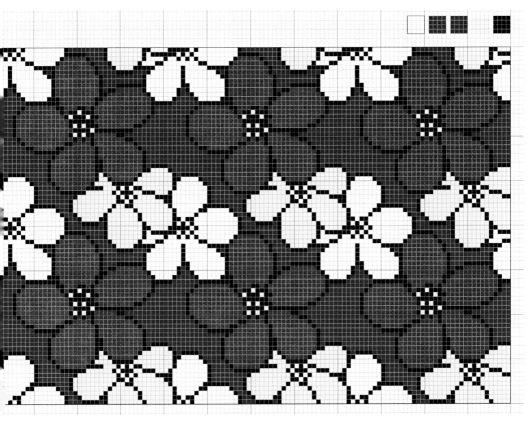

floral fantasy

FINISHED SIZE

■ Rug: 61 cm x 92 cm (24 in. x 36 in.) made up from six individual sections each 30 cm x 30 cm (12 in. x 12 in.)

YOU WILL NEED:

■ Latch-hook
■ Strong thread
■ Sharp sewing needle
■ Latch-hook canvas pieces for each individual section, 40 x 40 holes between selvedges, plus selvedge allowance
■ 6.5cm (2 ½ in.) lengths of rug wool in the colours below (packs contain approximately 160 pieces). I have multiplied this recipe by six to make it easier for you if you want to make the complete rug as charted.

INSTRUCTIONS

■ To bind as you hook, fold under four-hole width at each raw edge. Bind the selvedges through the double canvas at each end as you work.
■ Work in horizontal rows, following the chart carefully.
■ Turn under and sew bound selvedges to the underside of the completed piece. Finish as desired.

COLOURWAY 1			30 cm x 30 cm (12 in. x 12 in.)		61 cm x 92 cm (24 in. x 36 in.)	
Shade		Code	Lengths	Packs	Lengths	Packs
White		(36)	561	4	3366	22
Primrose Yellow		(21)	122	1	732	5
Apricot		(56)	247	2	1482	10
Tangerine		(42)	211	2	1266	8
Indian Orange		(41)	356	3	2136	14
Tan		(32)	103	1	618	4

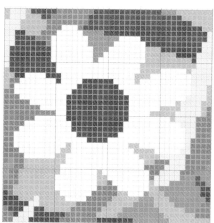

▲ 30 cm x 30 cm   ▼ 61 cm x 92 cm

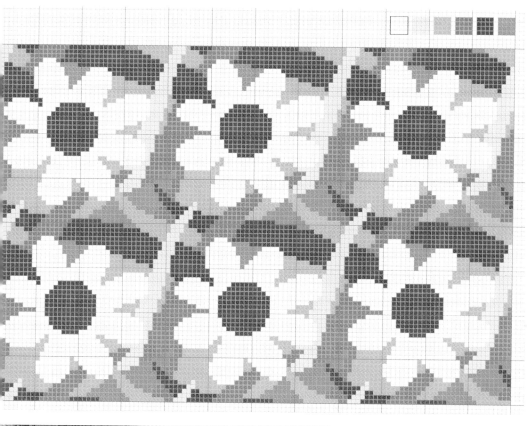

COLOURWAY 2			30 cm x 30 cm (12 in. x 12 in.)		61 cm x 92 cm (24 in. x 36 in.)	
Shade		Code	Lengths	Packs	Lengths	Packs
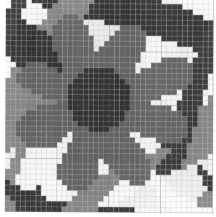 Bluebird		(74)	561	4	3366	22
Hydrangea Blue		(23)	122	1	732	5
Ice Blue		(12)	247	2	1482	10
Aqua		(45)	211	2	1266	8
Teal Blue		(25)	356	3	2136	14
Silver		(16)	103	1	618	4

▲ *30 cm x 30 cm*

104

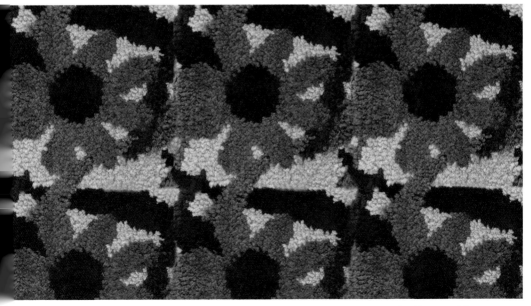

▲ *61 cm x 92 cm*

Monochrome Magic

Over the years, the use of black and white in interior décor has proved a popular choice. This is both a classic and powerful colour combination, which demonstrates a very confident, no-nonsense approach. Importantly, everything goes with black and white. I have included a selection of rug charts that fit into the category of monochrome magic – remember monochrome doesn't have to be monotonous.

spots and dots

Believe it or not I got the idea for this design after having been stuck in a dreadful traffic jam in the pouring rain. As the rain started these enormous splashes cascaded onto my windscreen and spots and dots was born.

FINISHED SIZE
- Rug: 61 cm x 92 cm (24 in. x 36 in.) made up from six individual sections each 30 cm x 30 cm (12 in. x 12 in.)

YOU WILL NEED:
- Latch-hook
- Strong thread
- Sharp sewing needle
- Latch-hook canvas pieces for each individual section, 40 x 40 holes between selvedges, plus selvedge allowance
- 6.5cm (2 ½ in.) lengths of rug wool in the colours below (packs contain approximately 160 pieces). I have multiplied this recipe by six to make it easier for you if you want to make the complete rug as charted.

INSTRUCTIONS
- To bind as you hook, fold under four-hole width at each raw edge. Bind the selvedges through the double canvas at each end as you work.
- Work in horizontal rows, following the chart carefully.
- Turn under and sew bound selvedges to the underside of the completed piece. Finish as desired.

Shade	Code	30 cm x 30 cm (12 in. x 12 in.)		61 cm x 92 cm (24 in. x 36 in.)	
		Lengths	*Packs*	*Lengths*	*Packs*
White	(36)	909	6	5454	35
Black	(48)	691	5	4146	26

▲ 30 cm x 30 cm   ▼ 61 cm x 92 cm

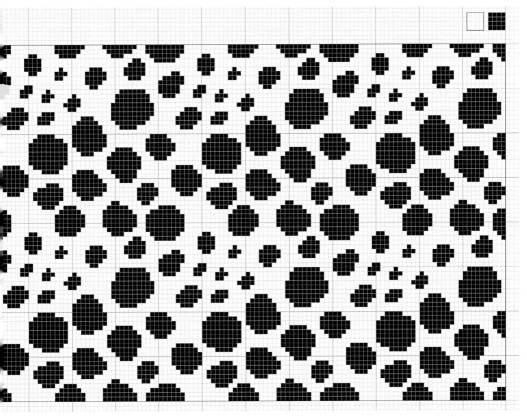

ripple

FINISHED SIZE

- Rug: 61 cm x 92 cm (24 in. x 36 in.) made up from six individual sections each 30 cm x 30 cm (12 in. x 12 in.).

YOU WILL NEED:

- Latch-hook
- Strong thread
- Sharp sewing needle
- Latch-hook canvas pieces for each individual section, 40 x 40 holes between selvedges, plus selvedge allowance
- 6.5cm (2 ½ in.) lengths of rug wool in the colours below (packs contain approximately 160 pieces). I have multiplied this recipe by six to make it easier for you if you want to make the complete rug as charted.

INSTRUCTIONS

- To bind as you hook, fold under four-hole width at each raw edge. Bind the selvedges through the double canvas at each end as you work.
- Work in horizontal rows, following the chart carefully.
- Turn under and sew bound selvedges to the underside of the completed piece. Finish as desired.

Shade	Code	30 cm x 30 cm (12 in. x 12 in.)		61 cm x 92 cm (24 in. x 36 in.)	
		Lengths	Packs	Lengths	Packs
White	(36)	681	5	4086	26
Black	(48)	919	6	5514	35

▲ 30 cm x 30 cm   ▼ 61 cm x 92 cm

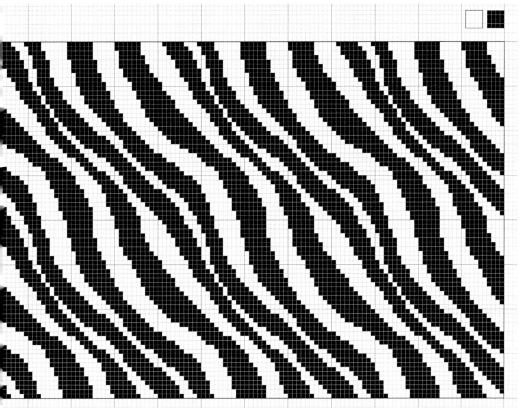

opposites attract

This developed after I had been playing with magnetic particles and a magnetic wand. Remember using magnetic particles to 'draw' shapes when you were a child?

FINISHED SIZE
- Rug: 61 cm x 92 cm (24 in. x 36 in.) made up from six individual sections each 30 cm x 30 cm (12 in. x 12 in.)

YOU WILL NEED:
- Latch-hook
- Strong thread
- Sharp sewing needle
- Latch-hook canvas pieces for each individual section, 40 x 40 holes between selvedges, plus selvedge allowance
- 6.5cm (2 ½ in.) lengths of rug wool in the colours below (packs contain approximately 160 pieces). I have multiplied this recipe by six to make it easier for you if you want to make the complete rug as charted.

INSTRUCTIONS
- To bind as you hook, fold under four-hole width at each raw edge. Bind the selvedges through the double canvas at each end as you work.
- Work in horizontal rows, following the chart carefully.
- Turn under and sew bound selvedges to the underside of the completed piece. Finish as desired.

Shade	Code	30 cm x 30 cm (12 in. x 12 in.)		61 cm x 92 cm (24 in. x 36 in.)	
		Lengths	Packs	Lengths	Packs
White	(36)	400	3	2400	16
Black	(48)	1200	8	7200	46

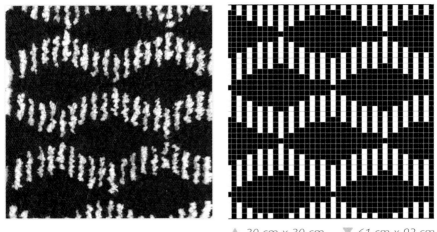

▲ 30 cm x 30 cm ▼ 61 cm x 92 cm

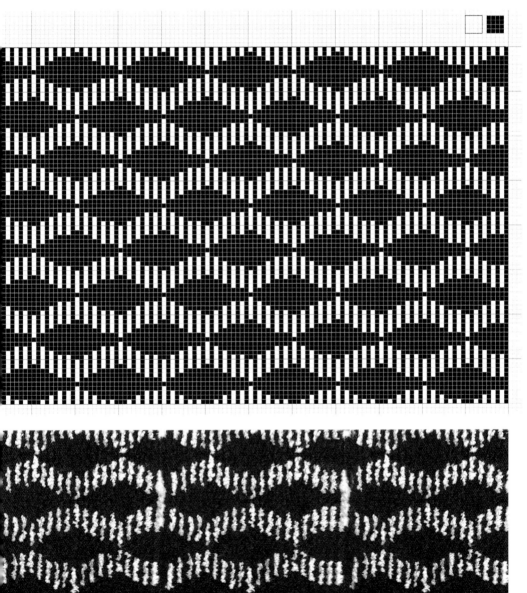

puzzle

I love puzzles and they are something we have always enjoyed doing as a family so I thought that I would include a puzzle design for posterity.

FINISHED SIZE
- Rug: 61 cm x 92 cm (24 in. x 36 in.) made up from six individual sections each 30 cm x 30 cm (12 in. x 12 in.)

YOU WILL NEED:
- Latch-hook
- Strong thread
- Sharp sewing needle
- Latch-hook canvas pieces for each individual section, 40 x 40 holes between selvedges, plus selvedge allowance
- 6.5cm (2 ½ in.) lengths of rug wool in the colours below (packs contain approximately 160 pieces). I have multiplied this recipe by six to make it easier for you if you want to make the complete rug as charted.

INSTRUCTIONS
- To bind as you hook, fold under four-hole width at each raw edge. Bind the selvedges through the double canvas at each end as you work.
- Work in horizontal rows, following the chart carefully.
- Turn under and sew bound selvedges to the underside of the completed piece. Finish as desired.

Shade	Code	30 cm x 30 cm (12 in. x 12 in.)		61 cm x 92 cm (24 in. x 36 in.)	
		Lengths	Packs	Lengths	Packs
White	(36)	800	6	4800	31
Black	(48)	800	6	4800	31

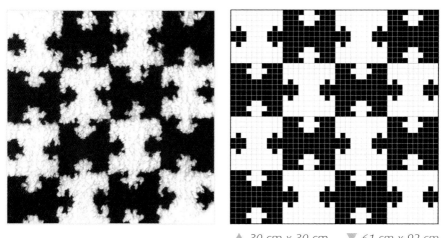

▲ 30 cm x 30 cm   ▼ 61 cm x 92 cm

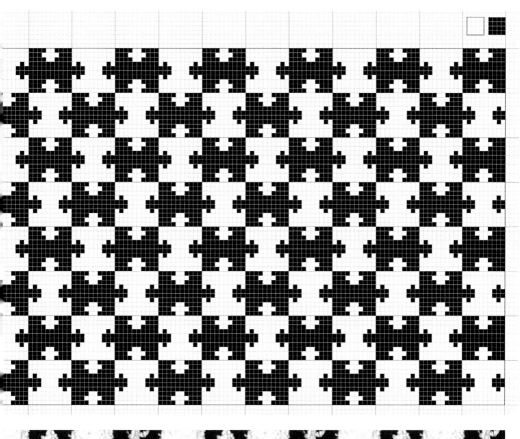

soon to bloom

Check out the colour version, Lazy Daisy, with the Bloomin' Marvellous rugs on p.98.

FINISHED SIZE
■ Rug: 61 cm x 92 cm (24 in. x 36 in.) made up from six individual sections each 30 cm x 30 cm (12 in. x 12 in.)

YOU WILL NEED:
■ Latch-hook
■ Strong thread
■ Sharp sewing needle
■ Latch-hook canvas pieces for each individual section, 40 x 40 holes between selvedges, plus selvedge allowance
■ 6.5cm (2 ½ in.) lengths of rug wool in the colours below (packs contain approximately 160 pieces). I have multiplied this recipe by six to make it easier for you if you want to make the complete rug as charted.

INSTRUCTIONS
■ To bind as you hook, fold under four-hole width at each raw edge. Bind the selvedges through the double canvas at each end as you work.
■ Work in horizontal rows, following the chart carefully.
■ Turn under and sew bound selvedges to the underside of the completed piece. Finish as desired.

Shade	Code	30 cm x 30 cm (12 in. x 12 in.)		61 cm x 92 cm (24 in. x 36 in.)	
		Lengths	Packs	Lengths	Packs
White	(36)	800	6	4800	31
Black	(48)	800	6	4800	31

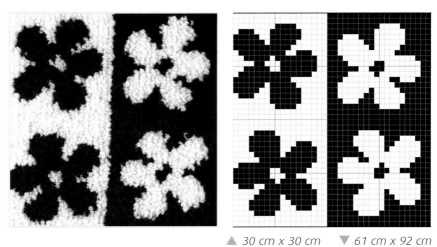

▲ 30 cm x 30 cm   ▼ 61 cm x 92 cm

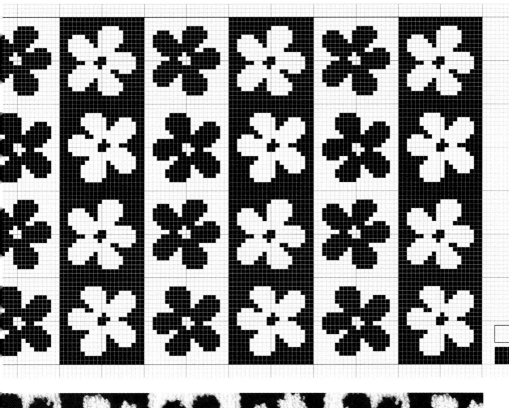

Monochrome Magic rugs

06
finishing

SEWING YOUR SECTIONS TOGETHER

Once you have finished all the sections, you will be ready to join the squares together. Make sure that your stitches will be as camouflaged as possible by trying to use the same coloured wool where you can, and by sewing each stitch beneath the knot.

1 Turn the squares face down. Match the rows of knots on the adjoining square and with the strong linen thread carefully sew the squares together.

2 Make sure that the stitches are sewn securely onto the canvas and not just onto the wool.

3 *Detail of stitching.* Secure the stitches at the intersection of the interlocking threads of the canvas, wherever possible.

4 The joined pieces.

Once you have sewn all the individual squares together, the outside edge can be finished off with a binding tape. Make sure that the binding tape is wide enough to cover the raw canvas margin and your stitching. Use small, evenly placed stitches and sew the tape as close to the edge of the rug as possible, making sure that it isn't visible from the top. I never feel the need to back completed rugs with a lining but you should feel free to do so if you so wish. Bear in mind, should you be considering lining your rug, that lining may serve as a very efficient dust trap. I don't use lining because I like to give my rugs a good old-fashioned beating every so often.

BINDING

RECTANGULAR AND SQUARE RUGS

1 Fold selvedge under and hold firmly. Using strong linen thread, stitch the selvedge to the underside. Make sure that the stitches are sewn securely through both layers of the canvas and not just onto the wool.

2 *Stitching to the underside: detail.* Wherever possible, secure the stitches at the intersection of the interlocking threads of the canvas.

3 Finish the outside edge with binding tape, making sure it is wide enough to cover the selvedge and your stitching.

4 Stitch one edge of the binding all around the outside edge of the rug. Make sure to catch the canvas as well as the knots. Hold the binding firmly as you work.

5 Finish by sewing the inside edges to the underside of the canvas.

6 Make sure you sew the binding securely onto the rug with small stitches, so that every possible square of the canvas is caught along both the outer and inner edges of the binding. This will ensure that your rug doesn't unravel during cleaning (in case your household is similar to ours and spillages are almost a daily occurrence).

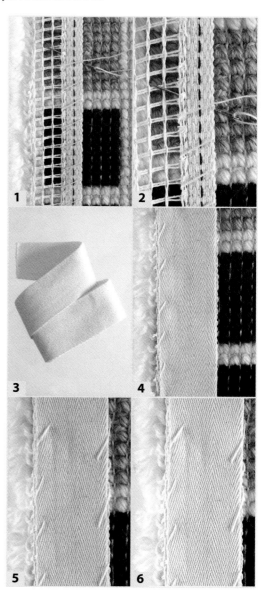

NON-RECTANGULAR RUGS

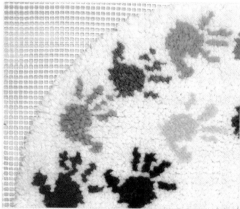

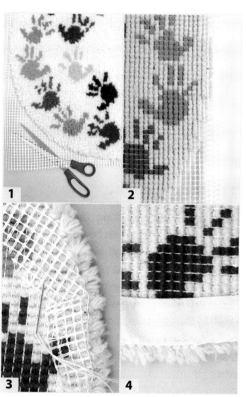

1. Do not trim the canvas until all your hooking is completed. Once you have finished hooking, cut your canvas to size leaving a border the width of the binding tape. To prevent fraying, trim only a small section at a time.

2. Fold under and stitch to the underside with strong linen thread.

3. Make sure that the stitches are sewn securely onto the canvas and not just onto the wool. Wherever possible, secure the stitches at the intersection of the interlocking threads of the canvas.

4. The outside edge can now be finished off with a binding tape. Make sure that the tape is wide enough to cover both the raw canvas margin and your stitching. Stitch one edge of the binding all around the outside edge of the rug. Make sure to catch the canvas as well as the knots. Hold the binding firmly as you work.

5 Finish off by sewing the inside edges to the underside of the canvas, making small tucks if necessary to help the tape follow an outside curve.

6 Make sure to sew the binding securely onto the rug with small stitches so that every possible square of the canvas is caught along both the outer and inner edges of the binding.

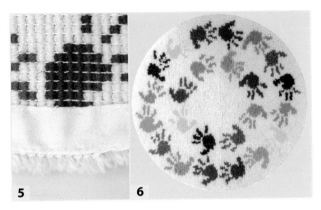

BINDING AS YOU HOOK

There are quite a few different ways to bind your rug once you have finished it. Standard binding techniques are described above, but binding while you work can be a less time-consuming method. For more information, refer back to p.15.

FRINGING

The value of adding a fringed edge to a rug is debatable. Even though they do look fabulous, particularly with beads on them, they are a bit of a no-no for our household. Cats and dogs enjoy nothing more than playing with fringes and of course a vacuum cleaner should never go near them, not to mention stiletto heels.

If you decide you can't bear not to fringe your rugs, all you need is fringing wool. You can customise the look of your fringe to suit individual rugs. The number of strands you use determines the thickness of the fringe; I recommend using two pieces per hole. Make sure that the fringing wool is a compatible thickness with the rug wool. Cut the fringing wool longer than you want the finished fringe to be; you can trim it when you have finished the fringing completely. There is no reason to just use one colour of wool – if you want a multicoloured fringe, use several different colours.

There is no reason not to go one step further – for a truly glamorous, sparkly rug, add beads to the fringing strands as well. Anyway, whether you decide to make a plain fringe, a decorative fringe or no fringe at all, the choice is yours as always but here are the instructions at last:

INSTRUCTIONS

1 Cut your fringing wool into 30cm (12 in.) lengths and fold two of these lengths in half.

2 Working from left to right, push the hook up through the first hole of the last row and catch the wool in the hook.

3 Pull the two lengths of wool through the first canvas hole of the last row of the completed rug.

4 Pull the four ends of wool across and place them into the eye of the hook.

5 Pull the four ends of wool through the loop, and gently pull to make a knot.

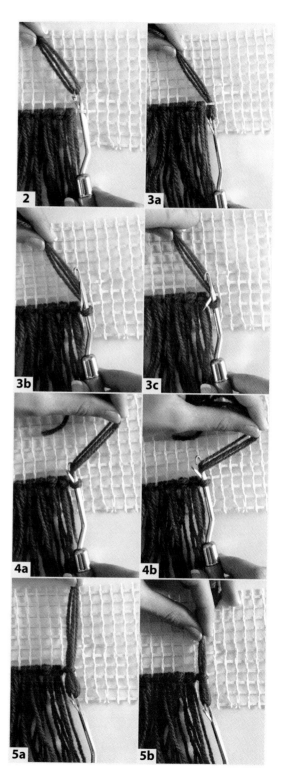

6 Repeat this procedure across all the remaining holes to complete the row of tassels.

7 Trim the uneven ends with a pair of scissors and you now have a neat fringe.

6a

6b

7a

7b

7c

8 Now turn to the other end of the rug and repeat the procedure.

oddballs: using up leftover wool

How about monochrome magic with a 'hint of a tint'? This means that the rugs are predominantly black and white but that you could add some colour here and there, or almost everywhere, like I have to transform 'Spots and Dots' into 'Oddballs'. The 'hint of a tint' method also helps to use up all of those leftover pieces of wool that are floundering at the bottom of your bag and can be incorporated easily into the monochrome designs. There is no guarantee that all of your left over bits of wool are going to look good when combined, so choose the wool carefully to see which colours work best. I have recommended and demonstrated using up my left over pieces with spots and dots because it is very easy to implement this method as the spots and dots come in varying sizes and are ideal for when you really have very few pieces of wool left over in any particular colour. By choosing your own colours, each and every spot and dot will be unique – although I have given you the recipe of the colours that I have used if you would prefer to reproduce it exactly. Remember, although the actual spots and dots only need left over pieces of wool, your background colour will need more.

oddballs

It might be that you have the same number of leftover wool colours as I do (although this is highly unlikely), or not, but I have given you the recipe for the wool colours that I have used anyway. Now is the time to play the game that I love so much: 'fit the leftover wool into the correct sized spot'. I have made it relatively easy for you to play this time by giving you stitch numbers. Have fun.

Shade	Code	30 cm x 30 cm (12 in. x 12 in.)		61 cm x 92 cm (24 in. x 36 in.)	
		Lengths	Packs	Lengths	Packs
White	(36)	909	6	5454	35
Black	(48)	177	2	1062	7
Biscuit	(2)	67	1	402	3
Stewart Blue	(10)	19	1	114	1
Silver	(16)	48	1	228	2
Spanish Yellow	(31)	42	1	252	2
Tan	(32)	31	1	186	2
Turquoise	(35)	39	1	234	2
Grass Green	(39)	19	1	114	1
Indian Orange	(41)	16	1	96	1
Aqua	(45)	19	1	114	1
Heather Pink	(52)	26	1	156	2
Apricot	(56)	6	1	36	1
Lavender	(61)	55	1	330	3
Lemon	(63)	10	1	60	1
Shell Pink	(72)	22	1	132	1
Sky Blue	(82)	6	1	36	1
Deep Coral	(93)	72	1	132	1
Emerald Green	(97)	10	1	60	1
Light Green	(614)	7	1	42	1

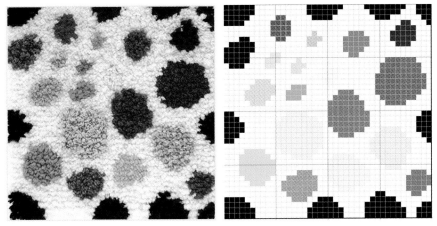

▲ 30 cm x 30 cm   ▼ 61 cm x 92 cm

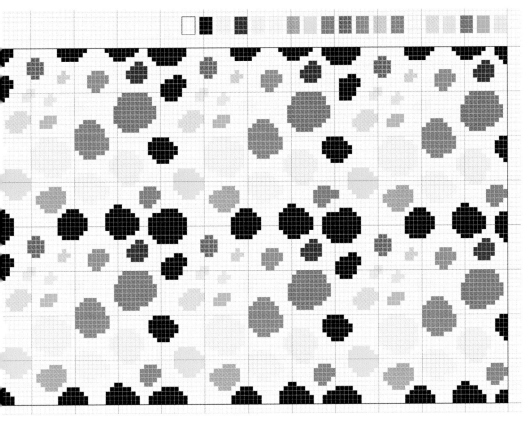

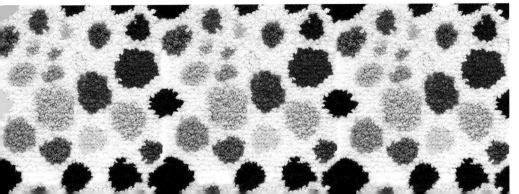

08
design and inspiration

INSPIRATION

For some of the designs I have added a little note about where my inspiration has come from. Either a small book of squared paper or a sketchbook is a 'must' to always carry in your pocket or handbag. It is invaluable to be able to 'jot' down ideas for future use, however roughly these are drawn. Carry a camera with you to be able to take that photo of whatever it is that has caught your eye. I think you will be surprised as to how often that camera is used. Making a scrapbook is a great way of being able to recall these ideas for future use, whenever that may be. I have lost count of how many times I have referred to my scrapbook which has also been filled with images that have caught my eye from magazines as well as ones that I have drawn or photographed over the years. You will see that even if you 'cannot draw' there are sources for design everywhere as long as you use your eyes. You can try:

- Collecting leaves, shells and pebbles whilst going for walks with your family.
- Watching sunsets when you are out walking the dog.
- Looking at architecture – both inside and outside of shopping malls, historic buildings.
- Paying attention to such detail as the curve of a garden wall.
- Flowers from your garden.

The list is endless. Above all keep your eyes and mind open.

DESIGN YOUR OWN RUG: CREATE A FAMILY HEIRLOOM

Now you have used some of my designs but you probably want to get on and do one of your own. You can take an image from a magazine (and print it out?) or you can go one better and what you might like to do is take your child's picture, a favourite photo or even your own artwork. It is a great gift idea for grandparents, friends and family members, especially to commemorate a special time or event. You will be creating a one-of-a-kind keepsake to be treasured and then passed down through the family. You might want to include other family members, or children, in the making process – everyone could have a go. The process of sharing a creative project is a great opportunity to get everyone involved in making something special that you can all be proud of. This is a really rewarding experience, great for family bonding and it creates some wonderful memories that will be rekindled through the years as you look back at the piece you all made together.

To create your own design, you can follow any one, or a combination, of the following steps:

1 Work out the complete scheme on graph paper, with one square of the paper representing one knot on the canvas.

2 Cut shapes and templates out of paper or cardboard. Place the cut shapes on the canvas, adjusting their positions until everything feels right, then use a pencil to trace around the shapes onto the canvas. Remove the shapes, and the general effect and proportions can be seen. Details can then be filled in either by eye or after drawing them first on graph paper.

3 Design as you hook. Some clever and talented people can achieve fantastic results working in this way, but for most of us I would recommend a combination of Steps 1 and 2 to ensure a finished design you are happy with.

INTERPRETING A CHILD'S DRAWING

Children's drawings can be an excellent source for original designs. Why not make one of your children's drawings into a rug? It's certainly an unusual and interesting heirloom. Rugs designed from children's drawings are fun to work on, and provide a lasting reminder of childhood.

Jack's original painting

The chart for this rug was created from six-year-old Jack's painting. The simplicity of the painting has translated well into the rug design, through the use of fresh, bold colours and strong outlines.

A chart of Jack's painting

▲ ▼ *46 cm x 76 cm (18 in. 30 in.)*

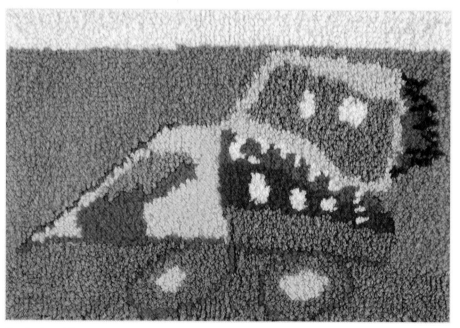

The Jackmobile

PUTTING A DESIGN ON CANVAS

There are various different ways to transfer your design onto canvas – experiment to find those that work best for you. Remember these instructions are simply to provide guidelines and some ideas to start you off.

DRAW

Draw your picture directly onto graph paper, allowing one square per canvas hole. With a pencil, roughly sketch your design onto the graph paper. When you are happy with the design, experiment with different colour schemes using coloured pencils or felt pens. Once you have decided on the colours, carefully outline the coloured areas in black pen. Remember to allow four blank squares at the rough edges for finishing. Choose wool to match your colours. Now you are ready to start hooking.

PHOTOCOPY

Photocopy the drawing you wish to translate and use a photocopier to increase its size to A3 in black and white. You only need the outlines at this stage – use coloured pencils or felt pens to colour it in later if you need to. Photocopying onto squared paper or graph paper will provide one of the simplest methods of drawing up designs.

PAINT THE CANVAS

Rather than referring to the chart every time you make a single knot, you may find it easier to paint the entire canvas with the colours before beginning the hooking. Acrylic paints are the best to use. They dry quickly, are diluted with water and have no smell and can be cleaned up easily and quickly with soap and water. Oil paints tend to take a long time to dry, are difficult to clean up and have to be diluted with offensive-smelling chemicals.

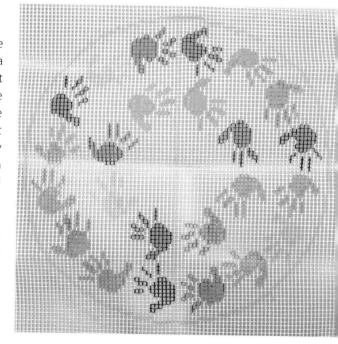

My nephew's handprints

I do not recommend using felt tip pens although this may seem like the easiest of options. Whichever method you choose, you should dilute the paint to a creamy consistency. Apply sparingly with an artist's brush and always allow it to dry completely before you begin to hook on the canvas. To transfer the design, you can always lay it underneath the canvas and trace over with paint.

leftsource.com

www.leftsource.com is a clever website that offers a great (free) service. You choose the size of chart you want, and the number of colours, then upload a digital image of the picture you want to hook, and the site provides you with a PDF of the chart as well as a colour list including the amounts you need of each colour. This is a lot of fun to play with and I find it a laugh to get an idea of what certain photos of people might look like if made them into a rug. The instructions on the website are incredibly easy to follow. Take a look yourself.

Rugs Designed from Drawings

houses

This is an adaptation of my original Houses painting.

FINISHED SIZE
■ Rug: 38 cm x 152 cm (15 in. x 60 in.) approximately

YOU WILL NEED
■ Latch-hook
■ Strong thread
■ Sharp sewing needle
■ Latch-hook canvas pieces for each individual section, 50 x 200 holes between selvedges, plus selvedge allowance
■ 6.5cm (2 ½ in.) lengths of rug wool in the colours below (packs contain approximately 160 pieces).

INSTRUCTIONS
■ To bind as you hook, fold under four-hole width at each raw edge. Bind the selvedges through the double canvas at each end as you work.
■ Work in horizontal rows, following the chart carefully.
■ Turn under and sew bound selvedges to the underside of the completed piece. Finish as desired.

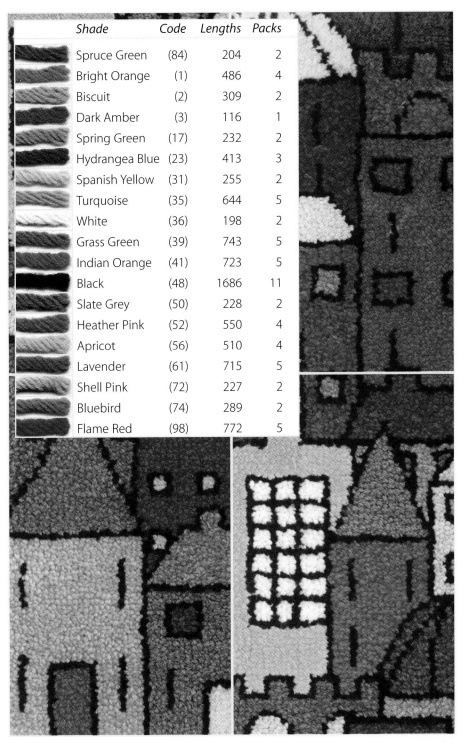

Shade	Code	Lengths	Packs
Spruce Green	(84)	204	2
Bright Orange	(1)	486	4
Biscuit	(2)	309	2
Dark Amber	(3)	116	1
Spring Green	(17)	232	2
Hydrangea Blue	(23)	413	3
Spanish Yellow	(31)	255	2
Turquoise	(35)	644	5
White	(36)	198	2
Grass Green	(39)	743	5
Indian Orange	(41)	723	5
Black	(48)	1686	11
Slate Grey	(50)	228	2
Heather Pink	(52)	550	4
Apricot	(56)	510	4
Lavender	(61)	715	5
Shell Pink	(72)	227	2
Bluebird	(74)	289	2
Flame Red	(98)	772	5

Houses (details)

131

dancing hands

What a lovely keepsake this rug is – as my nephew's hands seem to grow by the minute.

FINISHED SIZE
- Rug: 61 cm x 92 cm (24 in. x 36 in.) made up from six individual sections each 30 cm x 30 cm (12 in. x 12 in.)

YOU WILL NEED
- Latch-hook
- Strong thread
- Sharp sewing needle
- Latch-hook canvas pieces for each individual section, 80 x 80 holes between selvedges plus selvedge allowance.
- 6.5cm (2 ½ in.) lengths of rug wool in the colours below (packs contain approximately 160 pieces).

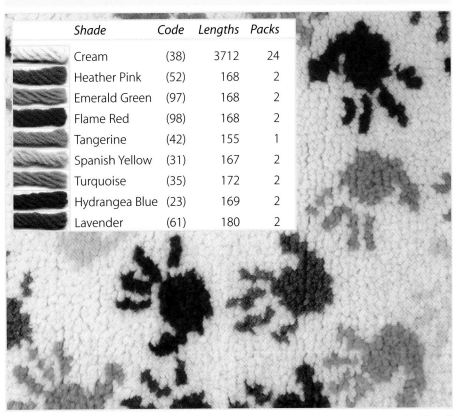

	Shade	Code	Lengths	Packs
	Cream	(38)	3712	24
	Heather Pink	(52)	168	2
	Emerald Green	(97)	168	2
	Flame Red	(98)	168	2
	Tangerine	(42)	155	1
	Spanish Yellow	(31)	167	2
	Turquoise	(35)	172	2
	Hydrangea Blue	(23)	169	2
	Lavender	(61)	180	2

Dancing Hands (detail)

INSTRUCTIONS

- Lay the canvas on a table with the selvedges to the left and right. If you are using a piece of canvas with raw selvedges, don't forget to put masking tape over the raw edges to stop fraying.

- Begin by hooking the shortest row at the bottom of the design whilst working in horizontal rows. Keep working in horizontal rows until you have completed the chart.

- Cut the canvas to shape, leaving a border of canvas that is the same width as the binding tape (approx. 4 cm/1 1/2 in.). Turn this canvas under and sew it securely to the underside of the finished piece. Sew the binding tape into position (see pp.118-120).

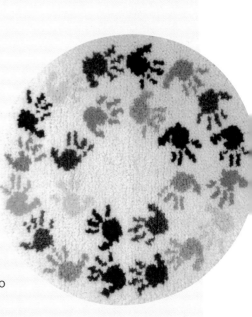

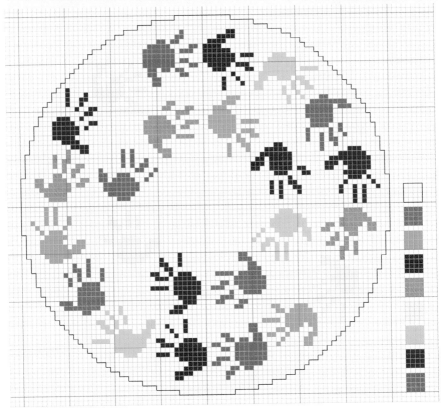

combining colours

Colour is my main inspiration – I absolutely love it. Colour is so important to me that I almost think of the colours for a rug before I think of the design, and the design of the rug develops from the particular colours that I want to use. There is no doubt that colour has a profound effect on most of us. I absolutely love the 'anything goes' look and believe that a bold colour or bright design makes a huge difference to the ambience of a room. I hope that my rug designs will motivate you makers into experimenting with more expressive colours.

The decorative nature of the room itself will determine the suitable colouring for your rug. A hot-coloured rug may draw attention to a gloomy part of a room or house as opposed to a light, bright beach house with white-washed walls which will make all but the fiercest coloured rugs seem dull. Dark rugs on dark wood or stone floors may to some seem to disappear and to others be a perfect match of tone and texture.

Remember the colourways that I have used for the designs in this book are only a recommendation and they can be part or fully substituted to complement your own interior. If you like one of the colourways that I have suggested for a striped design, but would prefer to hook one of the more geometric designs, there is absolutely no reason why you shouldn't substitute the two. Just be careful to keep a note of which original colour each new colour is taking the place of, so you don't lose track of where you are in the pattern and the amount of each colour you need. On pp. 138–139 you will find all the different colour combinations that have been used throughout the book.

colour chart rug

With this design I want you to use your imagination – I have given you only the colours and not the design. You can decide which colours to put to any of my designs or alternatively you can design your own rug and simply use the colour chart rug to guide you with which colours to use.

FINISHED SIZE
- Rug: 38 cm x 100 cm (15 in. x 39 in.) approximately

YOU WILL NEED
- Latch-hook
- Strong thread
- Sharp sewing needle
- Latch-hook canvas pieces for each individual section, 50 x 130 holes between selvedges, plus selvedge allowance
- 6.5cm (2 ½ in.) lengths of rug wool in the colours below (packs contain approximately 160 pieces). I have multiplied this recipe by six to make it easier for you if you want to make the complete rug as charted.

INSTRUCTIONS
- To bind as you hook, fold under four-hole width at each raw edge. Bind the selvedges through the double canvas at each end as you work.
- Work in horizontal rows, following the chart carefully.
- Turn under and sew bound selvedges to the underside of the completed piece. Finish as desired.

Shade	Code	Lengths	Packs
White	36	2704	17
Black	48	128	1
All other colours: each		64	1

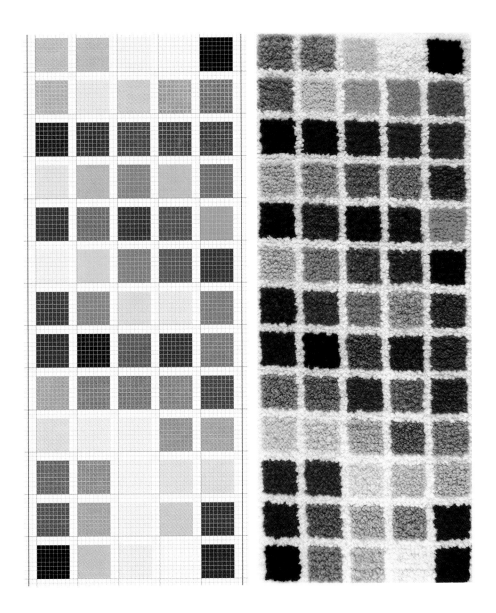

stripe tease
page 24
COLOURWAY 1

	Flame Red	(98)
	Heather Pink	(52)
	Turquoise	(35)
	Tangerine	(42)

COLOURWAY 2

	Sandalwood	(76)
	Loam Brown	(28)
	Light Sand	(87)
	Tan	(32)

stripe me down
page 30
COLOURWAY 1

	Biscuit	(2)
	Indian Orange	(41)
	Flame Red	(98)
	Cardinal	(65)
	Deep Coral	(93)
	Ruby	(60)

COLOURWAY 2

	Ice Blue	(12)
	Shell Pink	(72)
	Heather Pink	(52)
	Bluebird	(74)
	Lemon	(63)
	Pale Green	(614)

landing stripe
page 36
COLOURWAY 1

	Cardinal	(65)
	Navy Blue	(37)
	Light Grey	(29)
	Old Gold	(88)
	Biscuit	(2)

COLOURWAY 2

	Jade Green	(7)
	Spring Green	(17)
	Pale Green	(614)
	Evergreen	(22)
	Grass Green	(39)

stripe hype
page 42
COLOURWAY 1

	Hydrangea Blue	(23)
	Bluebird	(74)
	Ice Blue	(12)

COLOURWAY 2

	Heather Pink	(52)
	Shell Pink	(72)
	Pale Peach	(77)

stripe hype mixed
page 48

	Hydrangea Blue	(23)
	Bluebird	(74)
	Ice Blue	(12)
	Heather Pink	(52)
	Shell Pink	(72)
	Pale Peach	(77)

cross check
page 50

	Biscuit	(2)
	Old Gold	(88)
	Dark Amber	(3)
	Tobacco Brown	(26)
	Turquoise	(35)
	Aqua	(45)
	Teal Blue	(25)

check point
page 52

	Deep Coral	(93)
	Bluebird	(74)
	Light Grey	(29)
	Grass Green	(39)
	Biscuit	(2)
	Black	(48)

check your speed
page 54
COLOURWAY 1

	White	(36)
	Lavender	(61)
	Iris Purple	(54)
	Spanish Yellow	(31)
	Flame Red	(98)
	Black	(48)
	Heather Pink	(52)
	Emerald Green	(97)

COLOURWAY 2

	Grass Green	(39)
	Tobacco Brown	(26)
	Loam Brown	(28)
	Pale Green	(614)
	Mid Turquoise	(19)
	Bright Orange	(1)
	Deep Coral	(93)
	Biscuit	(2)

check mate
page 58

	Ice Blue	(12)
	Pale Green	(614)
	Oriental Gold	(44)
	Black	(48)
	Flame Red	(98)
	Hydrangea Blue	(23)

metropolis
page 62

	Lavender	(61)
	Bluebird	(74)
	Spanish Yellow	(31)
	Tangerine	(42)
	Flame Red	(98)
	Biscuit	(2)
	OR Black	(48)
	Emerald Green	(97)

sunset boulevard
page 66

	Indian Orange	(41)
	Flame Red	(98)
	Cardinal	(65)
	Tangerine	(42)

gridlock
page 68

	Bluebird	(74)
	Shell Pink	(72)
	Pale Green	(614)
	Heather Pink	(52)

mosaic mania
page 70

	Light Grey	(29)
	Tobacco Brown	(26)
	Black	(48)
	Cream	(38)
	Biscuit	(2)

sidestep
page 73
COLOURWAY 1

	Shell Pink	(72)
	Deep Coral	(93)
	Lavender	(61)
	Bluebird	(74)
	Spring Green	(17)
	Spanish Yellow	(31)
	Cream	(38)
	Oriental Gold	(44)
	Light Green	(614)
	Ice Blue	(12)

COLOURWAY 2

	Indian Orange	(41)
	Flame Red	(98)
	Tangerine	(42)
	Tobacco Brown	(26)
	Old Gold	(88)
	Silver	(16)
	Black	(48)
	White	(36)
	Dark Amber	(3)
	Biscuit	(2)

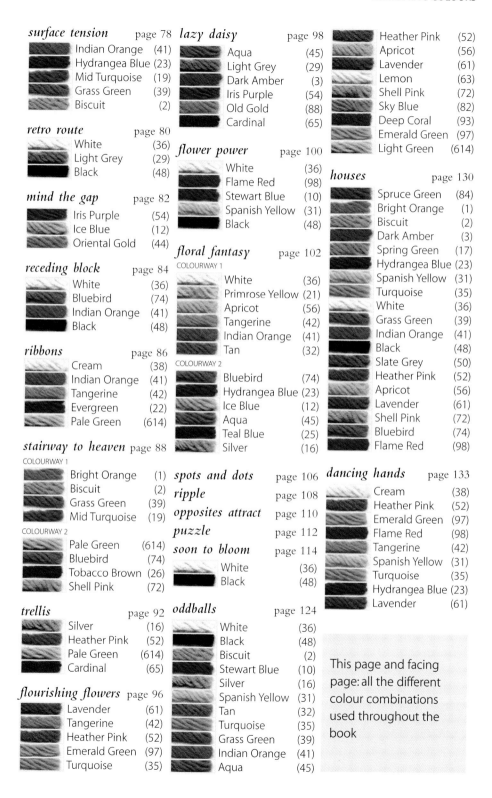

surface tension page 78
- Indian Orange (41)
- Hydrangea Blue (23)
- Mid Turquoise (19)
- Grass Green (39)
- Biscuit (2)

retro route page 80
- White (36)
- Light Grey (29)
- Black (48)

mind the gap page 82
- Iris Purple (54)
- Ice Blue (12)
- Oriental Gold (44)

receding block page 84
- White (36)
- Bluebird (74)
- Indian Orange (41)
- Black (48)

ribbons page 86
- Cream (38)
- Indian Orange (41)
- Tangerine (42)
- Evergreen (22)
- Pale Green (614)

stairway to heaven page 88
COLOURWAY 1
- Bright Orange (1)
- Biscuit (2)
- Grass Green (39)
- Mid Turquoise (19)

COLOURWAY 2
- Pale Green (614)
- Bluebird (74)
- Tobacco Brown (26)
- Shell Pink (72)

trellis page 92
- Silver (16)
- Heather Pink (52)
- Pale Green (614)
- Cardinal (65)

flourishing flowers page 96
- Lavender (61)
- Tangerine (42)
- Heather Pink (52)
- Emerald Green (97)
- Turquoise (35)

lazy daisy page 98
- Aqua (45)
- Light Grey (29)
- Dark Amber (3)
- Iris Purple (54)
- Old Gold (88)
- Cardinal (65)

flower power page 100
- White (36)
- Flame Red (98)
- Stewart Blue (10)
- Spanish Yellow (31)
- Black (48)

floral fantasy page 102
COLOURWAY 1
- White (36)
- Primrose Yellow (21)
- Apricot (56)
- Tangerine (42)
- Indian Orange (41)
- Tan (32)

COLOURWAY 2
- Bluebird (74)
- Hydrangea Blue (23)
- Ice Blue (12)
- Aqua (45)
- Teal Blue (25)
- Silver (16)

spots and dots page 106
ripple page 108
opposites attract page 110
puzzle page 112
soon to bloom page 114
- White (36)
- Black (48)

oddballs page 124
- White (36)
- Black (48)
- Biscuit (2)
- Stewart Blue (10)
- Silver (16)
- Spanish Yellow (31)
- Tan (32)
- Turquoise (35)
- Grass Green (39)
- Indian Orange (41)
- Aqua (45)

- Heather Pink (52)
- Apricot (56)
- Lavender (61)
- Lemon (63)
- Shell Pink (72)
- Sky Blue (82)
- Deep Coral (93)
- Emerald Green (97)
- Light Green (614)

houses page 130
- Spruce Green (84)
- Bright Orange (1)
- Biscuit (2)
- Dark Amber (3)
- Spring Green (17)
- Hydrangea Blue (23)
- Spanish Yellow (31)
- Turquoise (35)
- White (36)
- Grass Green (39)
- Indian Orange (41)
- Black (48)
- Slate Grey (50)
- Heather Pink (52)
- Apricot (56)
- Lavender (61)
- Shell Pink (72)
- Bluebird (74)
- Flame Red (98)

dancing hands page 133
- Cream (38)
- Heather Pink (52)
- Emerald Green (97)
- Flame Red (98)
- Tangerine (42)
- Spanish Yellow (31)
- Turquoise (35)
- Hydrangea Blue (23)
- Lavender (61)

This page and facing page: all the different colour combinations used throughout the book

hanging and displaying your work

Of course, not all of you will want to lay your lovingly-hooked rugs on the floor. Who can blame you? I have to say that I often end up wall hanging the pieces that I have made because the thought of someone walking all over my painstakingly made rugs, and leaving a trail of mud on them fills me with horror. There are so many different ways of hanging rugs onto the wall. I prefer to use either carpet gripper or Velcro depending on the weight of the rug. They both have the same advantage. The rug can be removed for cleaning or storage very easily. Having made so many rugs over the years, and often finding it hard to part with the finished item I find that more often than not when I take a rug down for vacuuming I invariably put another one up. I like to recycle them and seem to do this on a seasonal basis.

CARPET GRIPPER

This is normally used by fitters to invisibly secure carpet to the edges of a room and it is ideal for hanging larger and heavier rugs onto the wall. It is available in various lengths and can be bought from hardware shops. It can be either wooden or plastic and is covered on one face with small sharp pins (I prefer the plastic type). Cut the gripper about 1 cm ($\frac{1}{2}$ in.) shorter than the hanging edge of the rug and secure it with suitable fixings to the wall with the pins pointing outwards from the wall and upwards towards the direction of the ceiling. The rug should then be centred on the gripper rod and pressed gently but securely onto the pins.

VELCRO

Small, lighter rugs can be held onto the wall with Velcro. As with the gripper, cut the Velcro about 1 cm ($\frac{1}{2}$ in.) shorter than the hanging edge of the rug. Sew the more flexible of the two pieces onto the back of the rug. Even if you are using the sticky-backed Velcro

I still recommend that you stitch it onto the back of the rug. Staple the Velcro with the hooks either directly onto the wall surface (if your wall will hold it) or onto an exact sized batten that has been secured into the wall. Then all you have to do is press the two pieces of Velcro together and adjust gently to achieve your perfect hanging position.

CONCLUSION

When I sat down to write the introduction I couldn't believe that I was about to start writing a book – now I cannot believe that I am writing a conclusion for the finished book. I feel that coming to any sort of conclusion means that you have tested all the ideas and options along the way, and experimented to find the best for you; I am smiling as I type this because having written this book I feel that I have come to the end of a big adventure. I hope that your experiments with all the recipes and methods I have put together in this book have been successful and exciting as well.

Doubtless you have realised that there needs to be a touch of the fanatic about a hooker. So much is expected of you – organising, designing, counting accurately, double-checking, repeating patterns, careful finishing, commitment and so on. You need to find your own working rhythm, so that the process of making your knots actually forms a pattern of movements. I hope that, having completed a piece or two, you have discovered for yourself the great pleasure of hooking. Nothing compares to the personal satisfaction of having created your own rug. Hopefully my conclusion is your beginning.

SUPPLIERS

WEBSITES

Here are some websites that I have found particularly useful for information and supplies relating to latch-hooking. The UK suppliers will also post to Europe.

UK and Europe

www.coatscrafts.co.uk
www.readicut.co.uk
www.iriss.co.uk
www.sewandso.co.uk
www.sewessential.co.uk
www.knitandsew.co.uk
www.stitch1knit1.com
www.ethknits.co.uk

USA

www.spinayarn.com
www.latchhookrugs.com
www.alpineimport.com
www.knitcetra.com
www.leftsource.com

The internet is the most unbelievably valuable resource for those looking for information, services and products. I am sure that you will find what you need on one or more of these sites. Happy surfing.

ANCHOR RUG WOOL

All wool colour codes given through out the book are for Anchor Rug Wool shades. Your local craft supplier should be able to match similar shades from different suppliers if you prefer. Anchor Rug Wool is available all over the world – suppliers are listed below.

Australia

Semco Crafts
Unit 4, 7-11 Paraweena Road, Taren Point,
NSW 2229
Tel: (0061) 285 434 305

Canada

Coats Patons
Toronto, Ontario M6B 1B8
Tel: (01) 416 782 4481
Denmark
Coats HP A/S
Nannasgade 28, DK-2200 Kobenhavn N
Tel: (045) 35 86 90 37

Germany

Coats GmbH
79341 Kenzingen
Tel: (07644) 802 222

Spain

Coats Fabra, SA
08030 Barcelona
Tel: (93) 290 84 00

France

Steiner Frères SA
18500 Mehun-Sur-Yèvres
Tel: (33) 248 23 1230

Italy
Coats Cucirini Srl
20124 Milano
Tel: (02) 63 61 51

Portugal
Coats & Clark LDA
4431 Vila Nova de Gaia
Tel: (02) 3770 700

Switzerland
Coats Stroppel AG
5300 Turgi
Tel: (056) 298 1220

Sweden
Coats Expotex AB
51621 Dalsjöfors
Tel: (033) 720 7900

UK
Coats Crafts UK
Darlington DL1 1YQ
Tel: (01325) 394 394

USA
Coats & Clark
Greenville, SC
Tel: (800) 243 0810

INDEX